# CONTENTS

## Acknowledgements.

I love so many people in this world and I thank you for granting me the opportunity to lavish praise on a few special individuals who stand out and contribute so much to our world.

Carrie Sachse-Hofheimer is my hero. I was fortunate enough to be paired with her as a Peace Corps Volunteer over 30 years ago. Over these years we've worked hard alongside two beautiful humans, Huck and Milo, to create a better world. While I'm parsimonious with praise, Huck and Milo are exceptional members of the human race. Huck is kind, empathetic and funny. Milo is creative, mercurial and bold. If you were to draw a venn diagram of these three special people, you'd find an overlap around the adjective "humane".

I've also been lucky enough to have an "adoptive" daughter enter my life. Ruby Oliver is a fierce woman raising the most beautiful and funny girl, Amari Janai.

It goes without saying I wouldn't be here without my parents whom I lovingly refer to as the Costanza's. Joanie and Gilly gave me a great upbringing which provided the right balance of Jewish parent protection and latch-key kid freedom. My big sister, Betsy, was a constant source of humor...thanks Moose! I've also been fortunate to marry into the coolest family this side of the Mississippi: the Sachse's. I truly love all of my in-laws, nieces, nephews ... who can say that? Not a creep or a dud in the bunch, except maybe Dan Martier.

Over the years, I've been exposed to a variety of mentors even if they didn't know they were playing that role... thanks for the free and really good advice: Franck Schuurmans...rest in peace buddy...miss you every day (CUES), Mark Meyer (Filene), Kim Sponem (credit union CEO), Maurice Smith (credit union CEO), Lucy Ito (credit union CEO), Brian Schools (credit union CEO), Teresa Freeborn (credit union CEO), Mary Beth Spuck (credit union CEO), Linda Bodie (credit union CEO), Michael Neill (ServiStar), Taylor Murray (ServiStar), John Oliver (consultant), Dwayne Naylor (credit union CEO), Doug True (credit union CEO), Mike Schenk (CUNA), Linda Young (ponderpickle), Jamie Strayer (CU Strategic Planning), Doug Leighton (VISA), Joe Hearn (credit union CEO), Paul Walsh (some random Irish guy), Renee Saittewaite (AACUC), Lois Kitsch (Filene), Michael Higgins, Jr. (consultant), Denise Wymore (all the jobs), Fred Johnson (CUES), Richard "The Godfather" Pitchford ... RIP (Peace Corps), Sonny Askew (soccer coach), Scooter Scaggs ... RIP (soccer coach), Sam DeBone (soccer coach), Bill Reddan ... RIP (soccer coach) and Ian Barker (soccer coach).

As a functional introvert, I have a lot of acquaintances, but only a few really close friends. You all keep me fresh and happy even if we don't see each other as much as we'd like: (Uncle) Rickie Thomas, Dr. Jeremy Schiller, Dr. Eric Wollins, Josh Stamberg, Andy Rodin, Lora Dibner-Garcia, Dr. Bobby Canter, Michelle Boorstein, Greg Rossetti, Chris and Sarah, Sarah and Marty, Peter and Andrea, Matt and Kirsten, Brennan and Nate, Kerry and John (aka Victor), ITC members , and all the beer league and Sunday soccer guys...the dream is still alive.

We spend so much time at work and I've been blessed with amazing colleagues over the years, including: Sharon Swehla, Patsy "Bootsy" Stewart, Tansley Stearns, Ben Rogers (and Stevie!), Andrew Downin, Brent Dixon, Christie Kimbell, Denise Gabel, Mollie Bell, Elry Armaza, Beth Schnabel, Holly Fearing, Ryan Foss, Taylor Nelms, Paul Dionne, Josey Siegenthaler, Jeremy Tollefson, Josie Collins, Dan Hoover, Matt Davis and Annie Showalter to name a few.

Special thanks to Vicky Franchino for her ninja-like editing and proofreading skills. All errors and omissions are my own despite Vicky's best efforts and recommendations.

# CHAPTER 1

# HOW I CAME TO VALUE BANKING ON A HUMAN SCALE

*"I saw a bank that said '24 Hour Banking', but I don't have that much time."*

- Steven Wright

I grew up in the 1970s and 1980s in the suburbs outside Washington, DC.—the mean streets of Bethesda, Maryland to be exact. My mom drove a fake wood-paneled Pontiac station wagon which would be considered a classic today, but back in the '70s it was decidedly not cool. On the way to our weekly shop at the Giant Grocery my mom, my older sister and I would make a pitstop at the local community bank's drive-thru to get some cash for the week and the occasional deposit into our family's account. Small talk would ensue between my mom and the teller as the transaction was being completed. Then the magic moment: lollipops for me and my sister. As my mom burned a gallon of leaded fuel pulling out of the drive-thru, my sister and I would wave to the teller from the rear-facing folding seats in the back of the wagon. Repeat this scenario a few hundred times during my childhood and, not surprisingly, my initial impression of banking was free candy.

When I graduated from high school I also

graduated from the rear-facing folding seats to being the driver of a sweet, gray Mercury Topaz with gray interior and a luggage rack on the trunk, for, you know, luggage. The same tellers that were there in my childhood set me up with everything I needed for my college years: checkbooks, transaction registers, an ATM card (which was a new thing) and a list of phone numbers in case I got into trouble. This was the pre-Internet and post-leaded fuel era. My needs were basic: food, rent and the occasional case of Hamm's beer[1], but they treated me like I was a high roller. The banking goods turned out to be sufficient and got me through college without much financial strain.

Fast forward to a few years after college. I had some unique experiences under my belt, a few thousand dollars in the bank and, on the advice of my dad, I went to the same local bank for a car loan. In the intervening years, our community bank had been acquired by a regional bank and then a soon to-be-national bank. The people were different, the logo was different and the bank didn't quite seem like my hometown bank anymore. They had even done away with candy in the drive-thru and replaced them with Junior Banker stickers. Who wants to be a Junior Banker at age seven?[2]

At this time in my life, I had just completed a variety of international development gigs with such well-known organizations as the US Peace Corps, Price Waterhouse and the US Trade and Development Agency. I was in between jobs but my prospects were strong and I had enough money to buy a car outright. Still, I listened to my dad (remember that kids) and applied for a loan so I could establish some credit history. The requested loan amount was $5,000. I had my eye on a red, 1986 two-door Saab 900 with a manual sunroof, no luggage rack on the trunk. Pretty damn cool.

I was turned down for the loan.

The bank informed me that my debt-to-income ratio was 'off the charts'. As a proud graduate of the University of Wisconsin I understood if you divide any number by zero it is actually 'undefined' not 'off the charts.' Still the bank's automatons couldn't see through the equation and suggested I increase my income before I apply for another loan. The well-heeled haggling skills I picked up overseas didn't work on the uniformed bank staffer who kept pointing to the loan decision report on a glowing green monitor, "It says you don't qualify."

But that financial setback was temporary. I went on to a succession of jobs that paid a cool five figures a year and eventually established an impeccable credit score (my wife's score is still better than mine despite the fact we share the same exact financial lives...one of life's mysteries). Much of where I find myself in life today is due to good fortune that was largely beyond my control. I am a white male. I possess an undergraduate and graduate degree. I have always had the support of my family who benefited from several generations of wealth creation through home ownership. I have money in savings. I have no student debt thanks to an athletic scholarship.[3] I have health insurance. I have the American Dream.

In short, I am not the typical consumer in today's America.

## What The Typical American Consumer Faces

According to the Financial Health Network's Financial Health Pulse® 2022 U.S. Trends Report, 70% of adults in America today (approximately 176 million people) fall into their categories of "Financially Coping" or "Financially Vulnerable." These individuals are struggling to spend, save, borrow, or plan in ways that allow them to be resilient and seize opportunities over time.[4] Additionally, demographic factors such as educational attainment,[5] race/ethnicity and even the zip code you were born in are eerily strong predictors of individuals' financial vulnerability.

Even more compelling is Harvard University

professor Raj Chetty's groundbreaking work that illustrates, "90% of children born in 1940 grew up to earn more than their parents. Today, only half of all children earn more than their parents did."[6] In other words, for 50% of the population, the American Dream is likely out of reach. So, if I as a privileged individual can get poor banking service, what about the significant portion of Americans who can no longer count on the American Dream?

## Who Can Help In A Post American-Dream World?

Thankfully there are credit unions. I was introduced to this peculiar institution as a 17-year-old freshman at the University of Wisconsin-Madison in August 1988. Hundreds of eager freshmen formed a line that snaked around the corner of the now demolished University Square Mall to park their money in UW Credit Union (UWCU). I didn't quite know what to make of the scene. The credit union name threw me for a loop: it wasn't quite a bank, but it was bank-like. There was an informal feel to the scene which contrasted with my limited perception of banks. Little did I know the eventual impact credit unions would have on my life and my career. For the knowledgeable reader, this is a literary device called foreshadowing.

My first real job in the United States came ten

years after this first encounter with a credit union. I learned quite quickly through my job as the professional development manager at the Credit Union Executives Society (CUES) that credit unions were different. They operated on a not-for-profit basis, they were cooperatively owned by their customers (called members), they were focused on service over profits and they were small, but significant, players in consumer finance.[7]

In this role I got to know the people who ran credit unions, and they did not conform to the automaton nature of the bankers I had previously met. Instead they reminded me of George Bailey: stalwart members of the community, decent people, humble and dedicated to the mission of 'people helping people'.

At CUES, I was fortunate enough to run their 'institute' programs which prepared people for career progression up to the CEO gig. These institutes were run in conjunction with universities I could <u>never</u> have gotten into as an undergraduate (or graduate student): University of Pennsylvania, Cornell University, University of Virginia, London Business School, Oxford University's Said School of Business and Harvard Business School. For eight years I absorbed the world's leading business thinkers as they applied their knowledge to the credit union system in such areas as leadership, governance, strategy and operations. My knowledge of credit unions expanded in the context of the larger business world. I sensed an opportunity for credit unions.

This opportunity came into clearer focus once I left CUES. I was fortunate that the two people offered the job of research director before me at the Filene Research Institute[8] didn't take the bait. What resulted was 15 ½ wonderful years as the head of research (and eventually innovation, incubation and advisory services).  At Filene I was tasked with diving into the key challenges and opportunities facing the credit union system. On average we published 30 research projects per year on topics ranging from operations and finance to technology and product development. We conducted this research in conjunction with academics and other leading thinkers; the result was the world's largest (and growing) research library on cooperative finance.[9]  Much like my experience at CUES, Filene afforded me the opportunity to learn both inside and outside the credit union system. I was fortunate to learn and research alongside professionals from organizations as varied as Princeton University, Rand Corporation, University of Texas, Michigan State University and University of Arizona as they put credit unions under their microscopes.

**Getting To The Heart Of What Makes A High-**

## Performing Credit Union

One of my favorite groups of research studies teased out the characteristics of high-performing credit unions over long stretches of time. The research discovered the following key characteristics of high-performing institutions:[10]

1. Prioritize lending
2. Optimize capital
3. Manage expenses aggressively
4. Provide favorable pricing for consumers

Empirically it makes sense for high-performing institutions to have the aforementioned characteristics, but these data are descriptive outcomes. Yes, the debits and credits must equal but the variables that define which debits and credits go where and when and how are infinitely complex and shifting. An organization can't simply aim to meet these outcomes without understanding their internal capabilities, the external environment and a view of the future. So, while this research was illuminating, it didn't really help credit unions 'get there.' To achieve long, sustainable performance, you have to search and find the hard to define, and harder to explain, "X factor" for high performance.

In addition to my duties leading research at Filene, I had the unique opportunity to work closely with about 400 separate institutions applying research to their particular situation. The typical engagement would look something like this: I get a call from a CEO who read a recent Filene report and found it interesting. This CEO has been thinking about this topic and what it means for her organization. She asks me to spend some time with her, her senior team and her board members to discuss the topic and its implications for the credit union. So, I book a ticket to an exotic location like Dayton or Albuquerque, make a reservation at the nearest Hampton Inn and spend the weekend hashing things out with the team (I owe my family some serious penance for being gone so many weekends). Repeat this scenario hundreds of times, and I have the insights to catalog a set of patterns I've seen time and time again.

## Common Mistakes That Too Many Credit Unions Make

Those weekend sessions helped me to pinpoint the following as critical mistakes that are holding credit unions back:

Most credit unions do not have a differentiated strategy. Without a strong, differentiated strategy consumers won't likely have credit unions in mind for their next product needs.

Most credit unions struggle with eliminating legacy thinking/programs. By continuing irrelevant programming you add expenses to already high cost operations.

Most credit unions utilize confusing (and sometimes wrong) success metrics. As a result, credit union employees often find themselves doing the "wrong" things while still being rewarded for their behavior.

Most credit unions don't have a compelling problem they are trying to solve. Centering your operations around a compelling reason for being leads to a coherent set of actions and strategies.

Most credit unions try to emulate banks by measuring their success with traditional financial metrics. A real opportunity for differentiation by centering success around human needs.

As of August 2022, there were 5,029 credit unions in operation.[11] This came from a peak of 23,866 credit unions in 1969.[12] Accepted wisdom points to changing consumer needs, technology, regulation and the need for scale as the key reasons for the elimination of so many individual institutions. However, as April Clobes, president/CEO of MSUFCU, a multi-billion credit union, has reminded me, "We all started at the same place." In other words, most credit unions have an origin story which generally starts something like this: "In 1948 with $5 each and a loan for $123.20 from their local union, ten Dubuque Packing Company employees start[ed] their own credit union."[13]

Those ten employees from Dubuque Packing Company would be astonished to see their credit union today: 120,000 members in all 50 states and 26 countries and nearly $2 Billion in assets. Dupaco Credit Union is not particularly blessed with an amazingly robust local economy, nor do they offer a unique set of products.

A lot has changed since 1948 and Dupaco has made significant upgrades in technology and operations, but dig deeper and you'll see vestiges of the 1948 institution. For instance, they offer up a newspaper-like quarterly newsletter, they provide a generous patronage rewards program, they focus heavily (and measure) the financial well-being of their members and they led the rebuilding of downtown Dubuque with the rehabilitation of a five story, historic (and previously vacant) millwork building as their new headquarters and operations center.

So, what differentiates the thrivers, like MSUFCU and Dupaco, who grew to billions of dollars under management, from the survivors and the survivors from the disappeared institutions? I believe the answer is that they simply operate the credit union with the member-owner in mind. In short: **They operate on a human-scale**.

Operating on a human-scale means you are centered on the needs of people: members, potential members, employees, members of your community, and board of directors. In a world dominated by scale and technology, smaller community-based financial institutions, like credit unions, have the chance to serve more people (and serve them better) by making banking more human. This book presents a way forward that places banking on a human scale.

When I think back to my earliest interactions with banks there was something deeply human about the drive-thru encounters at that small community bank in Maryland. Something as inconsequential as a lollipop has stuck in my mind 40-plus years later. I saw firsthand the elimination of human scale operations as automation and more profit seeking took over the bank. These changes didn't create a better experience for me, the human/consumer. Credit unions have an opportunity to consider a more humane way forward and, as an outcome, better serve the nearly three-quarters of Americans who are financially coping, or worse.

**How This Book Is Organized.**

Banking on a Human Scale begins with the human in mind so I go heavy on the prose and avoid tables, graphs and charts, except for one notable exception in Chapter 4. I also include a variety of references via endnotes (some more useful than others ... and there are 231 of them!) and resources

GEORGE HOFHEIMER

that you or your co-workers can dig into deeper if interested at the end of each chapter. I regularly cover these topics with individual organizations I work with, so imagine you're at a Hampton Inn off Interstate 74 in Peoria, Illinois, grab some stale coffee and let's get banking on a human scale.

# CHAPTER 2

# START WITH THE CONSUMER

*"Human behavior flows from three main sources: desire, emotion, and knowledge."*

*- Plato*

The first time I saw Mark Meyer, the CEO of Filene Research Institute, work his magic was at the inaugural meeting of the i3 group[14] in Sedona, Arizona in 2003. If you've never met Mark, the best way to describe him is the mix of a whirling dervish, a corporate lawyer and Will Ferrell. Extreme energy paired with extreme competence. He operates at such a frenetic pace that it is hard for many to keep up with him. My former co-worker and, at the time, i3er, Denise Gabel lovingly ascribed his behavior as like a "fart in a skillet".[15] That imagery stays with me to this day.

In Sedona, Mark was staging the goals of $i^3$, which included building products, services and business models that would transform the world of consumer finance. The initial group of $i^3$'ers were accomplished (most are now CEOs), and had been through a screening mechanism that ensured we were dealing with the best of the best. Mark knew these individuals had brought ideas with them, but he urged them to forget these ideas now and "start with the consumer". Today the concept of human centered design is well-known and widely practiced; however, Mark's simple instruction set the stage for some breakthrough thinking that continues to this day.[16]

Starting with the consumer in mind helps narrow the focus of the problem you are trying to solve. This approach also allows accomplished executives to get outside their own head and experiences to examine a different viewpoint. As previously mentioned, today nearly two-thirds of people in America (approximately 176 million people) are 'Financially Coping' or 'Financially Vulnerable'. Most decision makers in credit unions today are certainly not living this type of financial existence. So, let's delve into the consumer's mind and make banking more human.

## Recognize That The Consumer Is Irrational

If anyone took a traditional economics class in college, chances are you had to make the following assumptions: people make rational assumptions about what they value and these people are always trying to maximize their 'utility'. For example, if someone wanted to lose weight, the person would study which healthy foods to eat (what they value) and adjust their diet (rational decision) to maximize their utility (lose weight). Easy! Well...not so fast.

According to recent studies by the Centers for Disease Control, "The age-adjusted prevalence of obesity among U.S. adults was 42.4% in 2017–2018."[17] Not so easy. Anyone with lived experience can point to myriad examples why this is so: the deliciousness (and easy availability) of high-calorie snacks, the difficulty of changing long-term eating habits, and, my favorite, the brain's desire to seek out short-term pleasure over long-term gain.

Banking consumers fall into the same irrational behaviors. Some doozies from personal experience include keeping my 1996 Subaru Outback on comprehensive insurance coverage for five years after paying off the car thereby paying more in premiums than my car was worth. Keep a largish nest egg of savings in my credit union just in case I needed access to cash resulting in approximately $25 in dividends over the course of ten years versus investing that same savings into a tax advantaged index fund account which could have seen my nest egg triple in size. In the words of Chris Farley, "Idiot!"

The point is consumers are not idiots[18], but, in the words of Dan Arielly[19], predictably irrational. If credit unions co opt this mindset wonderful things can happen. Rather than try to change consumers' behavior, they can anticipate how consumers will act and be there for the win. But how?

### How To Better Understand Your Irrational Members? Talk To Them.

Many resources exist that you can utilize on a simple and straight forward basis, but finding the irrationality in your members' minds starts by talking with them. Think about the last time you truly talked to your members. Not in a focus group where you likely hired an outside firm. Not during a phone conversation where you were resolving a problem or selling a product. Not during the lightly attended annual general meeting over the rubbery chicken cordon bleu with a side of room temperature green beans. Real conversations.

In 2006 Filene worked with a handful of credit unions[20], and their members, to answer the generic question, "why did you become a member of XYZ Credit Union"? Over the course of 3 months we visited 85 individuals in their home or place of work to gain an understanding of the overarching research question. We also asked detailed questions about how members deal with their finances. We discovered new insights that required a bit of extrapolation but led to clever insights. For example, one individual showed us how he paired his monthly bill payments with a bottle of bourbon at the kitchen table, because he found the process extremely painful. Another individual illustrated her elaborate system of hiding money from herself so that she'd have enough money for essentials at the end of each pay period. Finally, one participant admitted he had very little funds in the institution because he sensed the credit union was less sophisticated than the local and national banks. He admitted in the same sentence that his perceptions weren't necessarily true, but he had convinced himself of this sentiment.

These insights, all irrational in a classical sense, provided a peek into the consumer's mind resulting in a host of insights and ideas for the credit unions. You can identify similar insights and opportunities at your institution by considering the following action items:

1. Ask your staff that regularly interacts with members the following questions:[21]
   a. What frequent patterns do you see when talking with members?
   b. What is the 'craziest' thing you have heard from a member?
   c. What unique insight do you recently hear from a member?
2. Set up limited office hours for the CEO (or another senior executive) to interact with members on a regular basis on any topic they wish to discuss. Include food whenever possible.
3. Create a member advisory group that

regularly meets with a 'middle manager' at the credit union to discuss how the credit union is working with them. Middle managers are typically the most effective information source in an organization.[22] Additionally, middle managers may be more approachable than executives for most members.

4. Evaluate the applicability of a program like Intuit's "Follow Me Home"[23] that temporarily embeds staff in consumers' homes to gain a better understanding of how they use their products and services.

## Create A Rational Model To Serve Irrational Consumers

If we make the assumption that consumers will continue to act irrationally, how do service-based businesses build a framework to channel this irrationality? This conundrum is rarely discussed and the resulting credit union service experience is uneven for many consumers.[24]

Over the years, I've been in awe of a handful of researchers that present ideas that fit three criteria: actionable, practical and unique. Frances X. Frei, a professor of technology and operations management at Harvard Business School, fits that bill. Her 2012 book Uncommon Service remains one of the most influential service excellence guides for organizations like credit unions. Frei's genius is that she characterizes the state of affairs for most organizations' service approach by saying, "It's easy to throw service into a mission statement and periodically do whatever it takes to make a customer happy. What's hard is designing a service model that allows average employees— not just the exceptional ones—to produce service excellence as an everyday routine."

Let's assume for a moment that your credit union does not have the most exceptional service employees. I know it is hard to hold that fact in your mind but stay with me. *How might credit unions design a system whereby even the least exceptional (or most junior) employees thrive in serving irrational consumers?* Luckily, Frei has a framework that stands the test of time, technology trends and changing consumer needs which I summarize below.

Frei reminds organizations that they can't be great at everything so trade-offs are necessary in your service model. She encourages companies to *understand how consumers define excellence* in your offering set. I re-emphasize consumers and not you or your member experience team.[25] Finding these trade-offs involves working with a subset of members and non-members to generate a list of things consumers value, rank order their importance and validate your findings through traditional market research techniques.

Once you've discovered the triggers of great service in the minds of your members, Frei implores organizations to devise a model that prioritizes only the most important items. And you've got to figure out how your credit union is going to "pay" for this service excellence. The logic makes sense: you can't be great at everything, but for the things you are great at (and consumers value), you have to pay for this greatness somehow. Take my preferred hotel go-to lodging partner, Hampton Inn, as a simple example. I value convenient and affordable locations paired with simple and comfortable accommodations. Hampton provides this value consistently but with no real frills, except for a free "breakfast" and some go-go juice all day long. In return, Hampton charges a higher than average price per night at $121 versus similarly value-oriented hotels like Super 8 ($51 average price) and Comfort Inn ($95 average price).[26] Not surprisingly Hampton Inn is a bit more affordable than the Ritz-Carlton.

I have seen very few examples of credit unions making the explicit trade-off between customer value and price by aspiring to provide the highest level of personal services at the lowest cost. This approach is not sustainable for obvious reasons. A simplistic example helps illuminate what an effective trade-off might look like in consumer finance. Assume your members value convenience first and foremost. So, you build out an outsized number of branches, or remote delivery channels, that are open seven days a week from 7 am - 7 pm. Additionally, you create a world-class suite of digital tools that enable convenient services after the in-branch hours. These investments undoubtedly result in a high-cost operation at your credit union. In order to pay for the thing your members value most (convenience) you have to charge more than the competition. You will pay less on deposits and charge more for loans. Since members value convenience first and foremost they would be willing to pay for this service model.[27]

## Empower Your Employees

Your path toward creating a rational model for irrational consumers continues with empowering your employees. While we all think our employees are way above average (see Lake Wobegon), your service model should be so well designed and simple that even below average—or junior—employees consistently deliver great service. With relatively little training, fast food employees are able to provide the service their customers value almost from day one without much room to screw things up. You want a Butter Burger from Culver's? A pimply-faced, 16 year old on the job for a couple of days delivers the goods within a minute in an affordable and quick manner. How might your credit union similarly streamline your service model if that's what your members value?

## Train Your Members

Frei cleverly observes that in service-based industries, "your customers routinely wander onto the shop floor-unannounced-and tinker with the assembly line." To ensure your service model is not left up to the whims of irrational people, credit unions need to train your members how to use the credit union. If you were to take all the iterations of Starbucks' drink menu there are nearly 80,000[28] potential orders so they have created a new language for their customers to use to ensure a quick, caffeinated purchase.[29] In the credit union context, I have seen employees intercept members in the branch and show them how to use Interactive Teller Machines (ITMs) because their service model makes better sense using ITMs than tellers. Train your members!

## Use Products As Entry Points

The psychological impact of delivering the right product to the person at the right time is profound. Think back to a time when Netflix recommended that show you had never heard about which resulted in eight straight hours of entertainment binging.[30] Or the host of technology companies' anticipatory ordering systems that proactively send customers regularly consumed items when you're low on quantities. I find that a bit creepy, but some people like it.

Consumers purchase products much less frequently in financial services, and as highly regulated entities, product features and benefits are necessarily narrow. A conforming mortgage is a conforming mortgage. This is why entry point products are so important for credit unions to consider. Entry point products are exactly what they sound like: 'on ramps' to the credit union for new or low use members. In the introduction of this book I shared my first personal attempt at purchasing a financial product. As you may recall I was trying to buy a ~~used car~~ sweet red Saab for about $5,000. Financing a member's first, used car purchase is not going to make your credit union oodles of money; however, the psychological association with the institution will likely be extremely positive if you provide the right on ramp. Ask your management team, friends or staffers about their first used car. Chances are you will hear a glint in their voice describing the car (and associated adventures) and, if prodded, the associations with the financial institution experience.

Here are two common ways to provide entry-point

products.

*Solve a problem.*
Certain products are ideal entry points candidates. For example, "Employer Sponsored Small Dollar Loan" is a concept (re) pioneered[31] by North Country FCU in conjunction with Rhino Foods, a jewel of a small manufacturer in Burlington Vermont.[32] The product is simple: if a Rhino employee is in "good standing" they automatically qualify for an unsecured loan of up to $2,500. It is really a payday loan with lower interest costs and longer repayment terms. The loan is disbursed and repaid through the Rhino employee's paycheck thereby providing more security for loan repayment to the credit union. Rhino counts this product as a huge game changer for recruitment and retention of their employees, and North Country has a set of consumers that can now enter the traditional financial services world.[33]

*Be there for a life event.*
Other candidates for entry point products usually align with key events in the life of a consumer. Examples of such products I have seen in the market align with the following life events: birth of a child, getting married, leaving home for the first time, immigrating to the United States, going to college, getting divorced, joining the military, becoming an insurance agent, bar mitzvah, quinceañeras, obtaining a medical degree, and my

all-time favorite: buying your first used red Saab 900 with a manual sunroof.

## Explain How Banking Works

Try doing this with a friend or family member who doesn't know too much about banking: ask them what they think a bank does with the money they get on deposit. Chances are you will get a range of answers with the most likely one being some version of, "They put it in the vault." Most people don't understand the intricacies of how money flows in and out of your credit union. There is an enormous opportunity to change this state of affairs.[34]

One of the truly distinct things about credit unions is the circular nature of their business: Only member-owners can use the credit union's services. These members periodically deposit money into the credit union. Other members periodically borrow money from the credit union through other members' deposits. Most of your banking competitors cannot make the same circular claims so this is a true point of potential differentiation. There are infinitely more compelling ways to describe this flow of money concept to consumers[35] than how I just described the basic credit union business model. One such way comes from a cooperatively owned bank in the United Kingdom.

In 2001 I was the chief learning officer at CUES and we had just launched a high-level educational program for credit union board members at the London Business School. As part of the curriculum, the head of public affairs from the Cooperative Bank described their ethical policy.[36] This policy, which was first introduced in 1992, focused on top ethical concerns their customers had such as support of oppressive regimes, animal testing on cosmetics, the fur trade and blood sports.[37] Not your typical banking fare.

The genius of this policy was twofold. First, Cooperative Bank was one of the first financial institutions to explicitly state what they would NOT invest their customers' deposits on and they made a big deal every year touting the millions of pounds they turned away because certain lending deals didn't correspond to their ethical policy. Second, the public affairs team went very aggressive with their communication tactics. Rather than say, "Yep, we got an ethical policy, you should read it," they produced extremely provocative advertisements to describe why it was important.[38] One such video[39] shown in movie theaters in 1997, described their ethical position on landmines (I'm personally against them, too!). The advertisement's script follows:

*Touch the trip wire of the Val Mara 69 bounding landmine and ball bearings would be blasted through*

*those of you seated in rows A to G at over 1,000 miles*
*per hour, literally tearing you apart. Those in rows*
*H to L would be maimed beyond all recognition while*
*the rest of you would be left critically wounded. Val*
*Mara 69 landmines cost just 30 pounds each. Certain*
*regimes throughout the world borrow millions of*
*pounds in order to plant landmines indiscriminately*
*which is why one bank never has and never will*
*finance the supply of arms to oppressive regimes.*
*(fade to white dissolve of an explosion*
*and the Cooperative Bank logo)*

It is an understatement to say that this tactic opened up conversations with customers and potential customers about the flow of money. And I imagine this messaging is a bit different than your organization's attempts to communicate the 'credit union difference.' I recall Chris Smith[40], the head of public affairs at Cooperative Bank, saying something along the lines of, "...as a result of our ethical policy, people from all over the UK started asking themselves where is my money going and what is it supporting?" I use this example to illustrate the potential power of telling the credit union model (which is unique) in a compelling manner.[41]

If you are not into confrontational approaches remember credit unions are a lot like the previously mentioned character George Bailey in *It's a Wonderful Life*. His message was similar to the Cooperative Bank, "I don't have your money. It's in Tom's house...and Fred's house."  And it should be noted *It's a Wonderful Life* was named 'The Most Inspiring Film' of all time by the American Film Institute (AFI).[42] I have a few bones to pick with the AFI as *Rocky IV* does not even register on that list, but the sentiment is important: If you tell the credit union story correctly, you can inspire action in others. So, get out there and inspire your community. *Eye of the Tiger*, baby!

## Understand The Power Of Empathy, Reciprocity And Small Gestures

I like to have conversations with myself. These internal discussions help make sense of the world. Sometimes it's mundane stuff like 'what is my dog thinking' to more profound things like 'what moves or motivates people'? This more profound conversation grew out of observing extremely effective coaches, managers, mentors and family members in my life. The early lessons were formulaic but effective.[43]  As I grew in years and experience, I started to formulate my own philosophy:  The best member relationships are a potent combination of empathy, reciprocity and small gestures.

Let's use the textbook definitions[44] of each of these elements so we're all on the same page:

*Empathy* is the ability to understand and share the feelings of another person.

*Reciprocity* is the practice of exchanging things with others for mutual benefit.

*Gestures* are any actions, courtesies, communications intended for effect.

In my experience, credit unions get a "B" in empathy, an "A-" in reciprocity and a "D" in gestures. Take any of these items in isolation and you get a well-meaning but potentially ineffective result, combine them and you get something magical. Here are some examples of how credit unions can put this combination into action.

*Empathy*
Mortgages, an infrequent[45] but important consumer purchase, provide an excellent opportunity for credit unions to show empathy. For most consumers, a mortgage represents the biggest purchase of their life. The average U.S. mortgage is $453,000[46], which if put through the trusty Texas Instruments' calculator puts the member's total out-of-pocket purchase at well over $1,000,000, assuming a 5.2% interest rate. The mortgage process is complicated and daunting for both consumers and credit unions. Directly acknowledging the gravity of this purchase with your member costs you

nothing but puts you on the members' side. And the opportunity to establish empathy with this product is huge given the majority of U.S. credit unions' loan portfolio is in residential real estate loans.[47]

Credit unions have done a better-than-average job of empathizing with members about the complexity and importance of the mortgage process. In 2013, a Filene i$^3$ group created a product called Homease[48] which captured insights from the Domino's Pizza Tracker and applied those concepts in the labyrinthine mortgage process. This innovation has been built into pretty much every mortgage origination process today and is a great example of why I'd give credit unions a "B" in terms of empathy. What other ways can credit unions show empathy with their members?

*Reciprocity*
Reciprocity is built into the fabric of credit unions. They are mutual benefit organizations so the issuance of a mortgage comes from other members money and the repayment of a loan creates capital so that others can borrow funds for their purchases[49]. I'd give credit unions an "A-" in this area because (as noted above) they have not done a great job explaining the magic of this reciprocity.

If you truly want to supercharge this idea of reciprocity, here's an approach worth borrowing from American Airlines FCU.[50] They reward first-time borrowers for consistent on-time loan repayments with periodic drops in their loan's interest rate. The logic is simple. We're taking a chance on lending money to you, but if you're a good borrower we want to thank you for your actions by incrementally lowering your interest rate if you pay as promised.

*Small Gestures*
Credit unions nearly got a perfect grade on reciprocity, but they could do a much better job providing small gestures of gratitude.

This idea is not some form of new age thinking. Small gestures cost very little but can have an outsized impact.[51] That member with the $453,000 mortgage has been through weeks of back and forth with your mortgage loan officer, they've just come from (digitally) signing ludicrous amounts of paperwork to formalize the mortgage, then they (finally) get the key to the home. Rejoice! When's the next time this member hears from their credit union? A monthly statement is almost a certainty, but beyond that it's likely nothing. Small gestures can make a big difference.

What if after the mortgage closing the credit

union proactively sends a congratulatory pizza[52] to the brand-new homeowners? This member is going to pay the credit union hundreds of thousands of dollars over the next 30 years, is $20 going to help or hurt you? I'm certain you can think of infinitely more creative ways to build in small gestures to your service delivery model.

I learned the small gesture insight from my dad who was a car salesman back in the day. He was consistently the top sales producer at the dealership and quite frequently on a national scale. One of things he did early on in his career was build a DOS-based customer relationship management system[53] to keep track of his customers. One innovation he built into the system was a field for the customer's birthday and another field for the customer's date of purchase. On these two days he would deliver a handwritten note to the customer thanking them for their purchase and wishing them well. This simple gesture cost basically $0 but my pops contends it played a huge role in his sales success, which, incidentally, came mostly from repeat business.

**Next Steps**

The preceding section identified insights about consumers, the most important ingredient in the banking on a human scale equation. As potential next steps, I'd highly recommend the following set of resources for you and your organization:

Pick up a free copy of the Human Centered Design Kit from IDEO at https://www.designkit.org/ and apply it to your conversations with members

Listen to Melina Palmer's[54] weekly behavioral economics focused "Brainy Business Podcast" at https://thebrainybusiness.com/podcast/

Read Predictably Irrational by Dan Arielly

Read Nudge by Richard Thaler and Cass Sunstein

Read Uncommon Service by Anne Morriss and Frances Frei

Examine Filene Research Institute's Incubator at https://filene.org/do-something/incubator for ideas on entry point products

# CHAPTER 3

# RESEARCH APPROPRIATELY

*"Research is formalized curiosity. It is poking and prying with a purpose."*

*- Zora Neale Hurston*

Wwhen I became the research director at Filene Research Institute in 2005, I was the third choice for the slot. I had finished my MBA a few years earlier and had precious little experience in research except as a consumer of it. Even though I had a good understanding of credit unions, I was a bit of an unconventional choice.[55] To work around my lack of expertise we embarked on a new model of research centered around a blue- ribbon group of research fellows that would bring their research expertise and outlook to bear for the benefit of credit unions. Filene worked[56] with experts in governance, econometrics, decision science, operations management, financial engineering, consumer finance and a host of other areas. With this diverse group of experts we sampled ideas and approaches to some spectacular effect. Similar to the creativity of placing jello, imitation crab legs and a pepperoni pizza on a single plate at the Golden Corral buffet,[57] I learned that sampling different research models yielded some good results and some not-so-good results.[58] What follows are five major insights for the application of research in credit unions.[59]

P.S. I'm still not a researcher.

## The Scientific Method Still Has Value

You were likely introduced to the scientific method between the ages of 5-18. For me it was at Wood Acres Elementary School in 1977 on the bad side of Bethesda, Maryland. My 2nd grade teacher, LuAnn McKelvey, a ginger with limitless energy,[60] asked us to determine why one side of the classroom was always warmer than the other side. She provided a framework (the scientific method) via a mimeographed worksheet which looked something like this:[61]

1. **Wonder** — What do I want to know about the world around me?
2. **Think** – What do I think will happen?
3. **Act** – Test my idea. What happens?
4. **Say** – Am I right?

The approach was simple in 2nd grade and it should be simple for those running multi-million (or billion) dollar financial institutions. Unfortunately, I see very little of this practice in credit unions. It is not just credit unions: every organization I've been a part of rarely used the scientific method.

Maybe it's because the scientific method is viewed as too simple, or perhaps gut level decision-making is more en vogue today. Basically, "old" ideas are regarded as too basic for today's fast-paced, mission-critical, low-hanging fruit, enterprise-wide, client-centered business world.[62] I tend to trust ideas that have evolved from such thinkers as Aristotle, Rene Descrates and Francis Bacon and believe credit unions should too. A simple, low-cost approach[63] like the scientific method has myriad applications for your organization. A few things that you could be wondering about (and I've previously worked with credit unions on) include:

*Are members motivated more by price or service?*

*Is risk-based pricing an effective predictor of loan loss?*

*How much do members value credit union membership?*

In case you were wondering why my 2nd grade classroom had two temperature zones: we discovered, through the scientific method, that southern-facing windows brought in more sunlight (and heat) than north-facing windows. My original hypothesis, that the Montgomery County School Board was misappropriating their repair and facility funds, turned out to be false.

## Approximately Correct > Precisely Wrong

John Maynard Keynes is credited with saying, "It is better to be roughly right than precisely wrong." However, this assertion is only approximately correct as the original quote comes from a lesser-known logician and philosopher named Corveth Read.[64] Keynes popularized the quote due to his more imminent public stature.[65] Read was the steak and Keynes was the sizzle.

Research necessarily tries to be precise. Some disciplines are more inclined to preciseness, like the natural sciences although even this field has serious limitations.[66] Credit unions, as a research subject, fall broadly into the social sciences with such fields of study as economics, decision sciences and social relationships as the most important. For instance, the first research project I worked on at Filene was by a trio of brilliant researchers[67] looking to examine the impact of a CEO's leadership traits[68] on their direct reports' performance.

Like most academic researchers they presented the project through a massive number of data tables and reams of statistical regression analysis,[69] both of which could lead one to conclude a certain amount of precision in their findings. The researchers' deductions were strong but not conclusive. To quote the study, "CEO transformational leadership has both direct and indirect effects on VP [direct report] attitudes, and indirect effects on VP performance and organizational financial performance." Not a slam dunk but there was 'a there, there' that justified the effort.

This project, and hundreds of other research studies, cemented the importance of being approximately correct rather than precisely right or wrong. In short, when conducting research, hedge your excitement with reality.[70]

David Freedman, author of <u>Wrong,</u> supports this concept in an interview with *TIME* magazine, "Bad advice tends to be simplistic. It tends to be definite, universal and certain. But, of course, that's the advice we love to hear. The best advice tends to be less certain — those researchers who say, 'I think maybe this is true in certain situations for some people.' We should avoid the kind of advice that tends to resonate the most — it's exciting, it's a breakthrough, it's going to solve your problems — and instead look at the advice that embraces complexity and uncertainty."[71]

Freedman's perspective resonates because he values the importance of research...to a point. Be aware of research limitations, tap into the skeptic's mind and strive for being approximately correct. This type of thinking is not only applicable to research but all aspects of life. For example, raising children is the most delightful, confusing and sometimes maddening experience. Yet, if you were to peruse the numerous titles that provide simplistic parenting guidelines you might think there was a precise approach to raising your gifted child. Similarly in sport, there are numerous tactical approaches to success; however, as the philosopher-boxer Mike Tyson famously said, "Everybody has a plan until they get punched in the mouth."

Strive for being approximately correct, you'll be happy you did. Especially after that first punch in your mouth by the competition!

## Evidentiary Support

A corollary to the approximately correct maxim is seeking evidentiary support over ironclad data. I learned this insight from Peter Tufano, the previous dean of Oxford University's Said School of Business. At the time he was 'just' a professor at Harvard Business School, helping credit unions develop the concept of lottery-linked savings accounts through Filene's $i^3$ program.[72] The $i^3$ project showed initial promise so it rolled into a fairly large pilot program in the state of Michigan with the help of the state association. The goal of the pilot project was to see how the product worked at a handful of Michigan credit unions, so Tufano encouraged data collection that illustrated broad-based evidence that the program worked as advertised. I give him a tremendous amount of credit as he understood what moves industry versus any ironclad guarantee of statistically significant data. Today that product is known as *Save to Win* and is available in hundreds of financial institutions across the United States.

## N > 25 Yields Little New Insights

Many people assume quantitative research (e.g., surveys, manipulation of large data sets, etc.) is more rigorous than qualitative research (e.g., talking to humans). I find this assertion odd because most people I interact with in the business world find quantitative research confusing, boring, or some combination thereof. There is an imprimatur of sophistication to quantitative studies that says, "I did my homework, here is a big table of data, trust me."

I'm not here to trash talk this type of research, but to encourage heavier use of qualitative approaches. The major complaints about these approaches go something like this, "How can you find answers to our research questions by talking with a handful of people?" Point taken. Let me destroy this argument like I destroy the Golden Corral buffet.

First, qualitative and quantitative methods can

(and should) be used in tandem. For instance, say you want to discover the potential demand for a new product. Great! Start with a quantitative survey of target consumer needs. Next, take these insights and do some qualitative work testing the outcomes of the quantitative approach with real human beings. Finally, confirm your findings from both approaches in another quantitative study with something like conjoint analysis[73] to understand the ideal features of your new product. At the end of this process, you will only have an approximately correct answer to your research question, but you will have obtained the evidentiary support to move forward...Boom!

Some more good news about qualitative approaches. You don't usually have to talk to an enormous number of people to obtain useful insights. *Saturation* is a term used in research to describe the point in a (usually qualitative) study when "no new information is discovered in data analysis, and this ... signals to researchers that data collection may cease."[74] I know you're wondering, "So, how many people do I gotta talk to?" Well, like most things in research the answer is fiercely debated and it also depends on what you are studying. For those looking for an approximately correct answer, a good rule of thumb is 25 people.[75]

## Behavioral Experimentation Is Cool

ideas42 is an organization started by a group of behavioral economic geeks including the dreamy duo of Sendhil Mullianathan[76] and Eldar Shafir[77]. Eldar, a Filene Research Fellow, invited Filene's annual confab, big.bright.minds, to Princeton University a few years ago. The ideas42 staff conducted a 1 ½ day workshop on behavioral economics, which was well received by all in attendance.

Throughout the experience, Eldar and his team sprinkled in a series of behavioral experiments that were expertly built into the program without the knowledge of the 150 credit union executives in attendance. For instance, at the workshop sign-in, attendees were instructed to pick up their name badges as one typically would at a professional meeting. Then the attendees were asked to sign a waiver to permit ideas42 to use their likeness in marketing materials. Still pretty normal, right? However, when the attendees provided the conference staff their names, the ideas42 meeting staff said something along the lines of, "OK, let me search for your pre-populated waiver and nametag." The staffer then knelt behind a table to presumably get the form and badge, but what really happened was another staff member (usually of different gender and race) would pop back up with the materials for the attendee to sign, etc. You would think everyone would notice this shift. Well, the video never lies. At the end of the program, ideas42 staff showed the raw video of almost every attendee[78] missing the obvious shift.

ideas 42 conducted other experiments during this program including a mundane but potentially impactful example of so-called "hassle factors." Hassle factors are small inconveniences that can cause outsized impacts on consumers' behaviors. In their experiment, ideas42 put two jars of absolutely delicious (and expensive) chocolates at the back of the meeting room in front of either exit door. Since the room was packed, attendees had an equal chance of departing the room through each of the two doors. One of the jars had a twist top while the other had no top. By the end of the program only a small fraction of the chocolates in the uncapped jar remained while the capped jar was barely touched. The point of this experiment was to illustrate how something as small as a jar top can impact consumer behavior.[79]

These small behavioral experiments opened peoples' eyes to the manifold (and sometimes illogical) behaviors humans exhibit. This type of research is often overlooked as a tool in credit unions. Consumer finance is about the delivery of financial services to people, thus this vein of inexpensive research may be a good fit for your organization. Plus, don't you want to be cool, too?

## It's Time To Revisit Your Approach To Pattern Matching

Technology is both a curse and a dream. The dream part is fairly obvious to most: You can take a handheld, wireless device and with the touch of a single button on a screen have a dozen buffalo chicken wings arrive at your door within 30 minutes. Less transformational examples of technology's promise include predictive analytics, massive data storage and the remote delivery of financial services.

The curse part may be less obvious, or as *Scientific America* states in a recent article, "We may be making ourselves dumber when we outsource thinking and rely on supposedly smart tech to micromanage our daily lives for the sake of cheap convenience."[80] Examples abound: Can you drive to a new location without the help of GPS? Can you remember who played the lead character in *National Treasure*[81] without asking Alexa? When was the last time you went to the restroom without scrolling through Reddit or Fruit Ninja?[82] In short, we have never in the course of human history been blessed with more access to more information, but I sincerely worry that we are losing knowledge (and becoming dumber) along the way.

For credit unions this shift in the use of technology is wrapped in the promise of more efficiency. However, this claim may be a bit spurious as U.S. credit unions' operating expense is roughly the same as it was in 1991 with only a 10-basis point deviation over the past 30 years.[83] Technology will play an oversized role in the future of consumer finance,[84] but too much of a good thing may not be the best way forward. Credit unions have the opportunity to carve out non-technological experiments to make banking more human. Which brings me to the topic of pattern matching

The legacy of most credit unions (and banks for that matter) was lending according to the 3 C's: capital, capacity and character. The capital and capacity variables have been largely outsourced to the credit bureaus. We can debate around the edges of their usefulness, on average, the systemization of these data holds value for both consumers and lenders. Character, on the other hand, has gone by the wayside except for commercial loans where part of the lending process involves inspection and evaluation of the management team's abilities. Credit unions overwhelmingly lend to consumers, and, with a few rare exceptions,[85] totally automate the lending process without considering character, or more specifically, circumstances.

The following is a fictionalized (but approximately correct) example of a friend's experience with a credit union. This individual had a fairly large ding on his credit report because of $15,000 in medical debt[86] he incurred as an uninsured student at the local technical college three years earlier. At the time of his loan application, he was an emergency medical technician making $42,000/year with $2,500 in credit card debt, $900 in savings and a direct deposit with his credit union. His credit score (capital and capability) was 620. He was 28 years old and single. He wanted to buy a used car for $15,000. You have no information about his character. Based on your current lending criteria would you make a loan to this dude? If so, at what cost?

I'll cut to the chase and tell you this friend was turned down for the loan and referred by the credit union to a series of resources on improving one's credit score in the form of outdated PDF brochures. He got the same pamphlets in the mail and a follow-up call from a member service representative asking how his experience was. Since he's a passive aggressive Midwestern he gave the credit union an "8" on their Net Promoter Score. He eventually obtained the loan from the used car dealership's F&I department at approximately 15% APR, or a little over $500/month for a 2011 Subaru with 85,000 miles.

Now, what you don't know about this person is that his character is unimpeachable. His medical debt was incurred intervening in a foiled assault on a mutual friend. While he is an EMT today, he was just accepted to medical school in New York, and he makes some cash playing guitar on the weekends at the local pub. But how would you know those things? Your systems are engineered to find a credit score, and that's pretty much it. Credit unions have moved away from their legacy of character lending for a variety of really good reasons, but I can't help but think your credit union would benefit if it rediscovered this differentiated approach. With a human department, perhaps?

*Pattern matching is what you are currently doing with credit scoring.* You create a hypothesis of patterns in data, collect observed data and determine if your hypothesis is correct with said data. But what if you applied pattern matching to character? Since character is a lot more squishy than debt and income measures,[87] you will have to tap into the previous discussions on research methods and approaches. So, what might this look like in practice? Allow me to set up an experiment that you could run at your credit union.[88]

## A Test Of Character

Let's start with the hypothesis that the credit union is missing lending opportunities because they don't consider character in the credit decision-making process. To test this, randomly choose 25 members that apply for an automobile loan during a specific time frame at the credit union.[89] Supplement their loan application with a simple request, "Please share any information about yourself that you think is important in helping XYZ Credit Union make this loan." I'd provide examples of what applicants might wish to share including extenuating circumstances, unique qualities/experiences and future plans.

Then, I would gather a diverse group of five credit union employees representing lending, member service, finance, marketing and branch operations to review these 25 applications.[90] Finally, I'd track the loan performance of the people whose "character" put them into a loan approval when the traditional lending criteria did not. Repeat this process several times and you will likely identify a variety of patterns unique to the members you serve thereby resulting in a potential strategic advantage over other lenders in your marketplace. Of course, at the end of this experiment you'd want to test your hypothesis and report back on the findings.

## Next Steps

I started off as a relative research novice, but the past 15 years running hundreds of projects and experiments has afforded me a point of view. This point of view would likely disqualify me from most PhD programs but places me firmly in the applied research camp. Research for research's sake is a luxury not afforded to a competitive market like consumer financial services. But applied research? There are plenty of reasons to get behind that. To help convince you and others at your credit union of the value of research, I'd highly recommend the following set of resources for you and your organization:

Visit ideas42 for a host of ideas on research methods at https://www.ideas42.org

Dig into a variety of research topics and studies at https://www.ssrn.com which contains published and unpublished research on every topic under the sun.

Read <u>Wrong</u> by David Freedman

Examine Filene Research Institute's Research library at https://filene.org/learn-something/ reports for ideas on almost any topic under the sun.

# CHAPTER 4

# ARE WE APPROACHING INNOVATION ALL WRONG?

*"What if you mix the mayonnaise in the can, with the tunafish? Or... hold it! Chuck! I got it! Take live tuna fish, and feed 'em mayonnaise! Oh this is great."*

-Michael Keaton in Night Shift

I 'm a pretty easy-going person..However when I recently turned 50 I noticed a few changes. Besides the obvious body aches and low T-levels[91] I started yelling at cars that sped through my neighborhood.[92] My lovely wife felt this behavior was out of character, but also recognized we were living in a pandemic and chalked it up to the uncertainty around us.

One day my wife and I were on a walk during said pandemic. As we crossed a busy thoroughfare a car sped through the red light and almost hit us. On cue, I let out a string of profanities, which didn't do any good. Then I noticed at the same intersection a police officer who did absolutely nothing as he missed the whole encounter due to him looking at his mobile phone. As we walked through the crosswalk I emphatically stated, "What the f*** is wrong with you? Didn't you see that a**hole run the red light right in front of you and nearly hit us? Do your f***ing job!"

This, my wife recognized, was a problem. She's a former police officer and said, "If that was me, I'd bring you in for questioning, or worse." She continued, "You need some help." It was not a suggestion, but a command. For a few months I spoke to a mental health counselor who recommended a variety of techniques to quell my inner Hulk, one of which was writing down things that bother me, reflecting on why these things bother me[93] and consciously identifying ways to manage said things. Crazy, right?

Here's my list:
1. People that speed
2. Dogs that are outfitted with coats, hats, boots or really anything that anthropomorphizes them
3. People that make a heart sign with their hands on social media
4. Sports teams that play in domed stadiums
5. Celery
6. Business lingo

My counselor said I was weird and acknowledged that he could be spending his time more effectively with people that truly need help. So, I declared myself 'cured' and I'm back to 'normal.'.

This roundabout story gets me to Number 6 on my bother list: business lingo. We can all think of lingo that drives us crazy (scalable, core competency, synergy, win-win, etc.). For me it is the word 'innovation' which may sound uncharacteristic because of my past work in that field.

IBM, a purveyor of information technology and

a big contributor to the explosion of business lingo, perfectly captured the ridiculousness of innovation in the corporate world with an advertisement starring "Innovation Man". Here's the transcript from one of their adverts[94] with a woman dressed as a normal corporate worker and "Phil" the Innovation Man, a more than slightly overweight man dressed in a spandex superhero costume:

Woman: "Hey Phil, what's going on?"
Man: "Innovation Man!"
Woman: "Innovation Man what's going on"
Man: "Innovation workshop!"
Woman: "...And your job is..."
Man: "Kickoff the innovation agenda! Fire up the troops for innovation hence the 'i' for ideation 'i' for incubation 'i' for invigoration!"
Woman: "'i' for implementation?"
Man: "Oh, I knew I forgot something!"

IBM's clever video[95] illustrates how the business world fetishizes innovation (and other business terms) by masking what we are practically trying to accomplish. When you pull back the curtain on innovation it is simply a new and/or novel way to solve new and/or old problems. Full stop. Let me repeat that: innovation is simply a new and/or novel way to solve new and/or old problems. By making innovation more complicated[96] than it really is we might miss the opportunities inherent in this wave of thinking. Let's call stuff what it is, and, please, don't dress your dogs up as humans.

## First, Ignore The Details

Compliance people are easy targets when it comes to innovation. New and novel concepts tend to tear at the heart of compliance professionals because these concepts try to solve a problem that has yet to be solved. No playbook exists for how this concept fits with the current regulatory framework, nor does it predict how a regulator will react. Thus, the compliance person's reaction is swift and definitive: 'You can't do that'.[97]

To make innovation work in heavily regulated industries like consumer finance, you need to keep these 'blocking' voices at bay during the *beginning* of the innovation process.[98] So, first, ignore the details. Details are critical later in the process, but your initial work should gloss over all the death threats[99] to a new concept. The 'corporate antibodies' will eventually attack any new ideas, but keeping them at bay early on is an essential ingredient to successful innovation.[100]

During this glorious first part of the innovation process, the constraints of being in a regulated industry are thrown off. You can forget if what you are building is legal, you can tear down the patriarchy and, yes, you can even wear jeans every day, not just on Friday! My former colleague/boss Mark Meyer brilliantly captured this approach when he led the i$^3$ group. Meyer would demonstrate this by running from one side of a meeting room and exclaim, "Go to the edge" then he would sprint to the other side of the room, out of breath, and add the rejoinder, "Then pull back to reality." Go to the edge, then pull back to reality. Great advice.

Have you heard of the world wide web? Yeah, you have! It's that cool system of tubes, wires and knobs that provide information networks for such varied groups as academics, flat earthers and grandma knitting circles. The creation of this transformational network is a great example of public-private innovation, but the relevant part of its creation story begins in Switzerland at the **European Organization for Nuclear Research, or CERN**[101], in 1989.

A guy named Timothy Berners-Lee attempted to solve for "...the problems of loss of information about complex evolving systems and derives a solution based on a distributed hypertext system."[102] CERN was doing a large number of complex and important projects with smart people who stayed an average of two years. These smart people were fairly independent operators and had very little structure for how they might share information across units. Berners-Lee's proposal for a system of 'hypertext' attempted to solve CERN's mundane information management challenges. His boss read the proposal and noted on the cover page, "Vague, but exciting."[103] That is the reaction you should be looking for at the beginning of an innovation process.

Berners-Lee eventually created a meatier proposal the following year that was blessed by CERN and resulted in the first hypertext system in use. Numerous other parties improved upon this concept, including Marc Andresson at Netscape, to make the world wide web more than just hypertext. The point here is the first stage of the innovation process is critical and you are encouraged to withhold reality as long as possible. Then pull things back to reality.

## Recognize Innovation Is Messy

Costas Markides was a faculty member for CUES' inaugural Directors Leadership Institute at London Business School in 2001. Costas is originally from Cyprus and the accent in which he speaks English is mesmerizing.[104] His combination of verbal staccato and strategic pauses feels like you are watching a dramatic tennis rally at Wimbledon.

At the turn of the century CUES' program, Costas was giving a talk related to his wonderful book

*All the Right Moves*[105] and he said something that stuck with me to this day and it went something like this: "Innovation is messy; it is meant to be extremely inefficient."

Seeing those words in print can't begin to convey the truth of them, but it's a lesson I observed and experienced for over 20 years. Innovation cuts against the grain of what most business organizations value: certainty and control. Sure there is a lot of lip service paid to thinking differently and failing forward, but, real talk here, organizations reward things that are almost all related to financial and operational results . So choosing to engage in a process that is 'messy' and 'inefficient' has many points of failure.

Steve Jobs is often credited with creating a diagram illustrating the innovation process that looks like this:

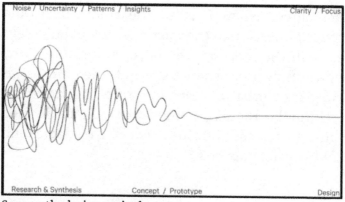

Source: thedesignsquiggle.com

Truth be told, the image was created by an illustrator and designer named Damien Newman at one of Xerox's R&D facilities in Cambridge, England.[106] Newman stated, "Their [Xerox's] process began with an abstract notion, through research moved to a concept and then finally ended with the design. So as I pursued my own career in design, I began to write proposals and pitch the process of design using the terms: *Abstract*, *Research*, *Concepts* and then *Design*. However, back then clients were only interested in the last bit: the design. Having no interest in any prior steps to the process. For them, as it was for many, design was the simple act of making ordinary things pretty."[107]

The so-called 'design squiggle' is a perfect encapsulation of what the innovation process will look like in your organization.

Remember when I asked the compliance (and other professionals) people to withhold judgment early in the process? I hope you understand why now: Innovation is not a straight-lined process, it is a giant hairball of stops and starts, zigs and zags. Eventually, though, compliance will be invited into the process and this is where the magic (and cold sweats) happens.

## Now, Add Constraints

It's fun to operate without constraints, ignore the details and get messy in an industry that is about precision and rules. But innovation is not a completely freewheeling exercise. At some point in the process, you need to tighten the focus, or as Mark Meyer says, "Bring it back toward reality."

This tightening of focus is exemplified in the design squiggle by the point where it looks like the hairball begins to untangle into a straighter line. There is no magic to this process; it's simply the introduction of the constraints credit unions are accustomed to.

The good news is that research has shown across a variety of different contexts (e.g., strategy, marketing, product development, technology, operations management, etc.) the introduction of constraints actually improves innovation outcomes.

What do we mean by constraints? Here are a few examples:[108]

*Time*: Deadlines are put in place for introduction of a prototype and delivery of a final product,

*Financial* resources: Unlimited budgets only exist for Elon Musk,[109] so you'll be constrained with less people, money and materials than you likely want,

*Process*: What was originally a rebellious,[110] no-rules project now gets put into the terminology of your organization (scrums, sprints and task boards, oh my!),

*Regulation*: Now is your time to shine, my much-maligned compliance people! Use your superpowers to poke the new beast and demand that no one will end up in an orange jumpsuit as a result of the innovation project,

*Design requirements*: Mold your prototypes and minimally viable products to the realities of your 1990s core processing system or wonky online account opening process.

Too many constraints, though, can stifle the creative process. A recent Harvard Business Review article stated, "... managers also need to be mindful about imposing too many constraints. When a creative task is too constraining, employees' motivation is hampered. If the space within which creative ideas are generated becomes too narrow, it is harder to form novel connections and serendipitous insights – both of which are vital for creativity. Hence, the key for fostering creativity and innovation in your organization is to strike a balance by orchestrating different types of constraints."[111]

The right balance between too many and too little

constraints is more art than science so remember that "'old' maxim: It's better to be approximately right than precisely wrong.

## Set Parameters Around What Success Looks Like

First, your organization should set up expectations about the level of success you expect in your innovation efforts. To get there, Google[112] offers a nice rule of thumb to consider when bucketing your innovation efforts:

70% is dedicated to *incremental* efforts by improving existing products with existing customers,

20% is focused on *adjacent* activities by expanding existing products to a new customer base,[113]

10% is driving transformational shifts by building products for markets that don't yet exist.

Each bucket will have a different set of expectations within your organization. For example, you would expect more wins in the incremental bucket than the transformational one. Similarly, the complexity and time to implementation would likely be higher for adjacent innovations than incremental efforts.

Fundamentally, the critical point of innovation is the implementation of new and novel concepts to solve new and old problems. Repeat as necessary until this realization becomes second nature.

## Recognize Innovation Without Implementation Is Zero

IBM's Innovation Man is similar to the many innovation efforts across the business, nonprofit and government sectors. People involved in these initiatives love the innovation process because they get to play in a sandbox that is different from the day to day of their professional lives.[114] However, innovation without implementation is kinda worthless. Sure we can espouse the benefits of failing forward or learning moments, but investment in new and novel ideas has to yield implementation of real world applications.

## What's Your Innovation Really Worth?

Think about the following formula when assigning the value of innovation in your organization: It should be an exponential function of its ability to be implemented.

$$value = idea^{implementation}$$

For instance, a million-dollar idea with poor

implementation[115] has a value of $1:

$$\$1 = \$1,000,000^0$$

Alternately, a hundred-dollar idea with exceptional implementation has a value of $1,000,000:

$$\$1,000,000 = \$100^3$$

I experienced the former more often than the latter in my innovation work, which is normal in a role where the goal is to have professionals come up with a lot of great ideas and then sort out their viability. But credit unions need to remember the critical point of innovation mentioned above: to solve new and old problems. And that means you have to find the sweet spot between 'cool' and 'viable.'

Here's an example of a great idea I thought landed in that zone.

Flex.One, one of the original $i^3$ product ideas, was created by a group of four individuals who are now CEOs of their respective organizations.[116] They described the product as, "...a first mortgage combined into a Home Equity Line of Credit (HELOC) with all the capabilities of a checking account. The member's entire loan is a line of credit, which allows the balance to be paid down when there is excess savings and withdrawn should those 'savings' be needed."[117]

The inspiration for this concept was the so-called offset mortgage available, at the time, in the UK and Australia. Ultimately the US regulatory environment and vendors' core processing limitations killed this concept before any type of implementation. The group involved in creating this concept has gone on to other amazing things; they'd likely admit Flex.One is worth about $1 today. Cool idea, but that and $7.50 will get you a Venti whipped latte with two shots of caramel these days.

## Remember: Good Innovation Is Boring

Elon Musk is a polarizing figure. Personally, I think he's a smart engineer and, at times, a brilliant entrepreneur, but as a human he's a major douchebag.[118] Despite my personal distaste of his personality, one of his initiatives I find especially intriguing is *The Boring Company* which constructs, "safe, fast-to-dig, and low-cost transportation, utility, and freight tunnels....to solve the problem of soul-destroying traffic."[119]

The double meaning of "boring" resonates with me because the act of boring tunnels is, well, boring, but, if properly executed, with brilliant engineering and business acumen, these tunnels have the potential to transform the way we all live and interact. The not-so-subtle nod to the double meaning of the company makes me think a bit more positively about Musk because I believe much of the really useful innovation--especially in financial services—should be boring.

Look, for example, at the "innovative" buy-now, pay-later companies like Klarna, Affirm and QuadPay, which all got darling treatment from the glossy media and, in some cases, billions of dollars of capital[120] from investors. If you are wondering what 'buy-now, pay-later' companies are, well, they provide the radically creative concept of installment payments to consumers for a wide range of products.[121] An old idea rediscovered for the Interwebs Age.

## A Boring Example For Financial Services

Let's take a closer look at the Employer Sponsored Small Dollar Loan (ESSDL)[122] I referenced earlier in the "Products as Entry Points" section as another example of boring innovations.

But first, a bit of history. In 2007, the United Way in Chittenden County, Vt., convened a group of employers to facilitate the development and implementation of workplace supports to improve employee productivity, retention, advancement and financial stability. Among the needs identified by this "Working Bridges" employer collaborative was a way to help the growing number of employees requesting high cost, payday loans.

To address the challenge, Working Bridges employers partnered with NorthCountry Federal Credit Union to design a small-dollar loan. These were a way to help employees within their select employee groups (SEGs) gain access to emergency cash, avoid the high cost of payday lenders, establish or repair credit, and begin to save.

ESSDL was first piloted at Rhino Foods, a specialty food manufacturer in Burlington, Vt., with over 100 employees. As noted earlier, Rhino is the manufacturer of cookie dough for Ben & Jerry's eponymous ice cream flavor, so the well-being of these employees is of strategic importance to America's national interest.

Under the ESSDL program model, loans of up to $2,500 are made available to the employees of participating companies based solely on the borrower's ability to repay, which is evidenced by length of employment in good standing, not credit score. The application process is simple, and the money is typically available to borrowers within 24 to 48 hours. Loans are repaid through payroll deduction and repayment is reported monthly to credit bureaus. After the loan is repaid, a deduction in the amount of the loan installment continues on an opt-out basis and is deposited into the participant's credit union savings account. Borrowers may only have one ESSDL at a time, with terms that range from 90 days to 12 months, and interest that ranges from 15.99% to 17.99% as an annual percentage rate.[123]

Participating employers pay a small fee (based on the number of their employees) to help offset the costs of administering the program. Employers also agree to market the program through company channels, confirm applicant eligibility, set up payroll deductions and inform the lender if a borrower is separating from the company.

Employers do not underwrite the loans and bear no responsibility for defaulted loans.
The chief lending officers are now saying, "So, it's a signature loan." The CFOs are now saying, "So, not much loan volume." The chief marketing officers are now saying, "So, not much return on investment." The board members are now saying, "So, we used to have this kind of loan back in 1955 when we were a sole sponsor credit union and bubble gum cost a nickel."

To which I reply, "Yep, yep, yep and yep."

On the surface, ESSDL is a turn-of-the- century character loan with small aggregate volume and miniscule returns, but here are the critical things: the product fills a vital need (that can help drive improved financial well-being) and can be an on-ramp product for a new set of consumers. In other words, this loan is a very boring innovation and should be considered as a model of the very kinds of innovation credit unions should implement.

## Innovation Requires All Kinds Of People.

Allow me to provide more color to the 'Elon Musk is a douchebag' statement. I also believe he's an obnoxious, anti-social, megalomaniac whom most of us would find to be an intolerable dinner party guest. But I would probably want Elon on my innovation team. I'd also want an introverted frontline staff member, a skeptical finance professional, a pencil-necked Six Sigma project manager and a creative marketer.

Keith Sawyer, a former video game designer and a current professor of psychology at the University of North Carolina-Chapel Hill, has written and spoken widely about the creative process. Sawyer hits at the fallacy that innovation is the work of a lone genius. He states in a relatively recent lecture, "It's [creativity] not about one person generating a creative product. Today, it's about groups of people coming together and doing things greater than any one person can do."[124] Another thinker in this space created a vibrant and practical model that credit unions will find useful in determining who sits at the innovation table. Edward de

Bono[125], an author, medical doctor, professor, game inventor, consultant and entrepreneur wrote a book called *The Six Thinking Hats*. It's quite a read, but here's the punchline: Get these six kinds of people at the table and your decisions/outcomes will be much better. Here's a bit more detail on these six thinking hats, which can either be role played or identified based on personality and/ or experience within your organization:

*The White Hat* is a neutral and objective player only concerned with facts, figures and data,

*The Red Hat* is a from the gut person who leans heavily on emotions,

*The Black Hat* is the devil's advocate who is always cautious and ready to point out what could go wrong,

*The Yellow Hat* is optimism incarnate, someone who seeks out the positive in any situation,

*The Green Hat* is creativity unbounded[126], an individual who explores new and novel concepts unfettered from most peoples' frame of thinking,

*The Blue Hat* is all about process and ensures the other five hats are playing their assigned roles.

This framework may seem cheesy,[127] but it can

be an effective guide for your organization as you delve into all those boring innovations and find the correct places at the table for your highly creative Elons, your process-oriented geeks and everyone in between.

## Next Steps

Don't get lost in the sauce. Innovation is simply about new ways to solve new and/or old problems—not some sort of mystical, quasi-other-worldly activity that only lone geniuses or MBAs can participate in. Innovation is a messy, inefficient process that requires all kinds of people at the table. The end result, especially in heavily regulated industries like consumer finance, should be a product, service or business that your friend, neighbor or family member will meet with an "OK" and a shrug but also use. In fact, that reaction is exactly when you know you're onto something when it comes to innovation. A few ideas to keep your interest in this critical long-term topic:

Not sure where to start? As good a place as any is to understand the trends and issues that will shape our society over the long-term. There are many prognosticators out there, most are charlatans, but I'd put a plug in for Singularity Hub,[128] the information site associated with

Singularity University.

Read <u>Six Thinking Hats</u>, <u>Lateral Thinking</u>, and <u>Creativity</u> all by Edward de Bono

Examine Filene Research Institute's innovation repertoire at https://filene.org/do-something/programs/innovationworkshops for help kick starting or improving your organization's innovation process.

# CHAPTER 5

# CONTRARIAN
# MANAGEMENT

*"First rule of leadership: everything is your fault."*

-       *A Bug's Life*

I became a father before I became a manager. I had a variety of jobs before I became a dad including a 6-year run as a soccer camp counselor keeping track of a bunch of seven-year-old ankle-biters and later managing a younger crew of counselors. But I didn't really manage during this or other early work experiences. I just did the job, went home, ate tons of pizza and repeated.

My first kid, Huck, was born in the mid-1990s. He was (and is) a delightful child (man).[129] As a young one he had long, curly hair paired with a kind smile. Huck was funny, cheerful and also a bit sensitive (still is). His sensitivity created a host of one-on-one discussions very early in his life that were more challenging than the typical kid questions of 'Why is the sky blue' or 'How much salt is in the ocean' or 'What will the Packers do when Brett Favre retires'.

I recall one such interaction, which centered around a problem he was having with a classmate that was long-running, unpredictable and confusing. It wasn't your typical bully situation, nor was it a 'kids being mean' scenario, but a real relationship conundrum with no good answer.

Huck being Huck, he first tried kindness and empathy. That didn't work. Next, he tried logic. Nope. Finally, he tried to change the setting (usually on the playground) but the classmate and he were still having issues. In what now seems like a typical interaction between manager and staff, he said something along these lines, "I'm having problems with my friend. I feel like we get along and work really well together, but every once and a while something happens out of the blue and we turn into enemies. Then the next day, or the next hour, it's back to normal and we're good. I've tried a bunch of different things that my teachers and you suggested, but nothing worked. What should I do?"

I was thinking, "I have no friggin' idea,"[130] but I had to call a quick audible so I replied, "Have you tried confusing your friend when this problem happens"?

Huck, "What do you mean confusing?"

Me, "Well, if nothing you've tried works. Why not do something really confusing or completely absurd that changes the mood or the subject? Kind of like shaking an Etch-A-Sketch."

Huck, "Really bad analogy pops. Can you give me a better example?"

Me, "OK, so you and your friend are in class. Everything is going well, then something happens and he turns on you. Right?"

Huck, "Yeah, like yesterday Ms. Brown gave us an assignment. My friend and I were finishing a worksheet together, then all of sudden he stopped working and blamed me for finishing the worksheet."

Me, "Right"

Huck, "Then he gets super angry until the bell rings, then we are best buddies on the playground."

Me, "So, try this next time," I say, having no idea if it will work. "Ask your friend if he likes peanut butter and potato chips on a sandwich."

Huck giggled.

Me, "Or if this kind of thing happens on the playground ask him if he's ever been to Kalamazoo or Timbuktu"

Huck, "Are those real places?"

Me, "Yep, both are very exotic, too."

Huck, "OK, I'll try that but will it work?"

Me, "Dunno."

Luckily it did. Changing the subject created a shift in perspective, which somehow made Huck's friendship with his classmate more stable. Huck reported back the next day that his friend thought the off-beat questions were hilarious. This reaction egged Huck to ask even more creative (and age-appropriate) questions of his friend including topics related to Pokémon characters and the school principal's stinky underwear.

To this day I have no idea why I suggested this approach, nor why it worked. But it got me thinking about acting in contrarian ways. Not like storming the U.S. Capitol contrarian, but from a people management perspective. Since I was getting to that point in my career where co-workers and actual humans started relying on me in a formal manner I had to figure out how to 'manage' people. My staff would pose questions similar to the one Huck did when he was a wee lad and I had to be ready. What follows are some of my favorite aphorisms around management. Some of these themes may be new; some may be well worn. But taken together I've found them to be useful.[131]

## Flow

Have you ever been involved in a task and

become so focused that you lost sense of time and performance peaked? I experienced this during a handful of soccer matches in my youth. Later in life, I occasionally had this feeling in the workplace, most notably when working with individual credit unions during their strategy sessions. Oh, and of course everytime I'm with my wife.

I became curious about this sensation because it felt good and coincided with that rare occurrence of 'peak performance.' I got the chance to learn more in the early 2000s when I was at CUES. CUES hosts a program that is still in existence today called *CEO Institute*, which prepares senior leaders for the top position in their organization. It was during a session with Alec Horniman,[132] a CEO Institute faculty member, and a full professor at the University of Virginia, that I first heard a name for what I'd experienced: "flow." Horniman didn't come up with this term or its underlying theory, but he did a great job explaining it in real terms.

Flow is a theory put forth by Mikhil Csikszentmihalyi,[133] who recently passed away but was a longteim professor at Claremont College. He described it as follows, "During flow, people typically experience deep enjoyment, creativity, and a total involvement with life."[134]

Flow, it should be noted, is a fairly rare phenomenon and getting to this state of being at work can be especially difficult. Long-running data from Gallup[135] indicated only about a third of employees are considered "engaged," with engaged defined as "...those who are highly involved in, enthusiastic about and committed to their work and workplace." Sigh.

How can you create an environment where flow is more likely to occur? Let's imagine a situation where one person has the potential to experience flow, let's call them the employee, and one person could enable flow, let's call them the manager. For the employee, things like their skill level in a particular task and the difficulty of the task are key factors in achieving flow. Flow is most likely to occur with a highly skilled individual engaged in a highly difficult task. Managers, on the other hand, have a practical role to play, which is to offer the three fairly logical things to their employees:

*Sense of control:* Managers remove any barriers that would prohibit your employees from completing their task.

*Unambiguous feedback:* Managers provide timely and honest critiques of employees' performance.

*Clear goals:* Managers set and communicate what success looks like in a practical manner.

When it comes to managing people, we tend to complicate things with well-meaning systems, software and other corporate practices: read control. The three components listed above can go a long way to providing clarity and focus without all the confusion surrounding most corporate internal planning efforts. With no malice towards my friends in HR/performance management,[136] the following checklist may suffice for most people reading this book:

1. *Manager question:* Does your employee have the skills, knowledge and behavior to successfully complete their job? Yes __ No ___ Maybe ___. Provide specific examples.
2. *Employee question:* On a scale of 1-5 (1=many --- 5= none) how many barriers exist that make it difficult for you to do your job? Provide specific examples.
3. Employee question: On a scale of 1-5 (1=never --- 5= always) my manager provides timely, relevant and actionable feedback. Provide specific examples.
4. *Employee question:* I understand the goals of my job: Yes __ No ___ Maybe ___. Provide specific examples.
5. *Employee question:* Do you like peanut butter and potato chips on a sandwich? Yes __ No ___ Maybe ___. Provide specific examples.

Compared to most performance management programs, this approach is simple, does not require some sort of fancy/expensive human resources information system[137] and aligns with a framework that most organizations would like to achieve. Imagine the richness you could get out of this five question framework if you implemented it on a quarterly basis. Instead, most organizations are left with compliance-driven[138] systems which measure too much, tend to be complex and generally don't address or change behavior.[139] While not completely contrarian, this approach provides a simple, humanistic approach to people management. Something we can all get behind, right?

**Pressure Is A Privilege.**

The first time I was invited to speak professionally was in 1999 for the CUES' Iowa Council in Pella, Iowa. My assignment was to talk about CUES' institute programs and why they would be a good fit for the 20 or so assembled credit union senior executives.

I was scared shitless.

The last time I had spoken in front of an audience was six years earlier as a Peace Corps Volunteer at the technical college I taught in a regional capital of Uzbekistan. For that speech the expectations were really low. All I had to do was get up for five minutes in front of the college's administration and talk about how wonderful the town, school and students were...in the Uzbek language. The audience knew me well from an unending series of invitations to local weddings, after-school vodka drinking sessions with the college's rector and hours and hours in the faculty lounge laughing about livestock jokes. But Iowa was different, I wasn't yet fluent in credit union-ese, these were executives I knew only by reputation, and I felt completely out of my depth. CUES' CEO at the time, Fred Johnson, assured me I was ready, but in retrospect I think he just didn't want to drive to Pella, Iowa. Fred had all the leadership chops: he was an Army ranger, former West Point instructor and retired executive from Bell Labs. As I trotted out of his office into my rented Chevy Impala Fred said, "I wouldn't assign this trip to you if you weren't ready."

I was still nervous, but after the four-hour drive, I checked into the Baymont Inn,[140] went to the pre-conference happy hour and did my thing. Everyone from Iowa is nice...really nice.[141] They treated me like a returning war hero which put me at ease, along with the couple of beers I consumed. The session started and ended, I was complimented and drove back through the cornfields to Madison, Wisconsin, a self-conceived returning management guru.

Of course, I was nothing of the sort. The real magic was Fred who gave me the platform to succeed, which leads me to the great philosopher: Billie Jean King.

King, as many of you know, was a champion tennis player. She is also a leading voice for the LGBTQ community and was the subject of the movie, *Battle of the Sexes*. Oh, and she's part owner of the Los Angeles Dodgers and the Los Angeles Sparks of the WNBA. She's a badass. King's book, *Pressure is a Privilege*, catalogs her life experiences and hits on the thesis that, "pressure is a privilege...it's what you do with it that matters." This sentiment resonates because many people are given growth opportunities, which cause varying degrees of personal 'pressure'. According to King, that pressure is a privilege because you've been put on a platform to show your stuff. What people do with that privilege is where the magic comes in.

Brent Dixon, a good friend and former colleague, realized this formula when he built what is now known as *The Cooperative Trust*. Back in 2011 Brent recognized[142] the need to lift the next generation up through a series of events known as "crashes"[143] where young professionals could come to industry events, meet the leaders of the credit union system and go back home to apply lessons learned. Each individual is interviewed to determine their readiness for this type of experience and are sent a list of expectations for their time as a "crasher". Therefore, the Cooperative Trust acts as a platform for these young leaders to put them in a 'pressure' situation. Of course, not all crashers take full advantage of this pressure platform, but many do. A handful made serious networking connections to advance their career. The platform is the starting point. From that platform comes pressure. And from pressure...well that is up to the person what they do with it.

Managers can play a transformative role in determining when someone is ready for the pressure and providing a platform to do something about it. Think about those platforms in your organization, community and industry. It's probably the best professional development and mentoring program out there.

## Weak Signal Tracking

We are blessed to be living in a time where information is ubiquitous. Can't remember who played the police chief in *Fletch*? Ask Alexa and she'll reply, "Joe Don Baker played Chief Karlin in *Fletch*, the 1985 film which is widely regarded as the best movie ever made. Would you like to learn more about Joe Don Baker's acting career?" The younger generation who has grown up with these technologies are generally unimpressed with this amazing set of circumstances, but I find it astonishing.

As mentioned earlier, this access to incredible technology and data is also making us a bit more stupid. We tend to associate access to information with knowledge and, as a result, we think we know more than we really do. From a managerial perspective we may be atrophying in some mental skills which previously allowed us to mull over data and try to make sense of it. With so much information at our fingertips[144] we simply don't have the time or capacity to tease out non-obvious insights. Instead, we are on to the next bit of information and the next and the next, until we find ourselves at 3 am scrolling through startled cat videos on YouTube.

Paul J.H. Schoemaker,[145] an expert in the fields of strategic management and decision making, conducted a recent report with Filene[146] to determine how credit unions performed in identifying and acting upon so-called 'weak signals' in this sea of data. We need to be appropriately skeptical of these results because credit unions were asked to self-report their performance in a host of managerial performance areas,[147] but the research[148] provides a great guide for your organization to see things sooner, and act faster. Schoemaker, for example, encourages managers to do a bunch of things,[149] but these two stood out:

> *Listen to and invite the lunatic fringe, mavericks and contrarians (!!) into your organization, and*

> *Use black hat people (!!) to question deeply held assumptions in your organization.*

## A Practical Example To Chew On

In 2016, I was assigned to help a credit union evaluate its strategic plan. As an outside contrarian[150] I was instructed by the CEO to treat the existing plan with little to no respect. I did my best Rodney Dangerfield impersonation to which the CEO steelily paused, stared me down and continued, "It's not that it is a bad plan, it's just that we [the senior team and board] are too close to it to know if it is good, bad or indifferent."

With such a broad assignment, I went into full black hat mode and asked senior- and middle-managers where each of the assumptions in their plan came from. For instance, was the assumption based on data? If so, where did the source data come from? If not, was the assumption a directive from the CEO and/or board? Did some assumptions come from a vendor who may have ulterior motives and/or incentives misaligned with the credit union? Most leaders would find it difficult to ask these types of questions to their peers and bosses...unless you encourage contrarian and black hat thinkers into your organization.

Next, I presented the CEO with a list of additional internal and external facts and figures and asked her to explain how these data impacted the veracity of the credit union's strategic plan. I was a bit sneaky by inserting some superfluous data as a sort of logic test.[151] She expertly digested the data and provided her thoughts, which in some cases supported the plan and in others caused her to pause and question if the credit union had missed something in their analysis.

Finally, I took all this information and wrote up a report which I later presented to the credit union's senior management and board of directors. My conclusions were, "You all have done a great job, and here are three things you may wish to consider to improve your plan." It doesn't matter what those three things were. What mattered was the process of stress testing assumptions, (re) analyzing new/old data and bringing in appropriately antagonist viewpoints.

The organization discounted two of the suggestions, but dove deep into the final suggestion, which was based on an overlooked data point in the Net Promoter Score (NPS)[152] data set. This organization had a high overall NPS, so they put less attention on this metric, and, as a result, didn't examine data outside of the topline NPS. "Hidden" within the data was a weak signal indicating a mounting consumer dissatisfaction with the organization's mobile tools. They didn't need me to find that data, but oftentimes organizations drift from an objective mindset to a more narrow one based on the various activities within the organization. In this case, the credit union had invested in a set of digital tools several years earlier and had severe implementation problems which were dealt with swiftly. Since that time, the management team assumed, after months of positive feedback, that the problem was solved so they stopped giving this topic high priority status. It's natural to let these types of things slide after an adverse experience, however, exceptional managers will allocate some time to those on the lunatic fringe (or in this case an outside advisor) to identify weak signals.

## Incentives Are Busted

What's your favorite song of all time? Mine is *Backstreets* by Bruce Springsteeen. Anytime this song comes on the radio[153] I belt out the lyrics:

> *One soft infested summer, Me and Terry became friends. Trying in vain to breathe the fire we was born in. Catching rides to*

*the outskirts. Tying faith between our teeth.*
*Sleeping in that old abandonded beach*
*house, getting wasted in the head, and hiding*
*on the Backstreets..*

The song conjures images of my youthful trips to the Delaware Shore[155] with my goofy high school friends, especially the 'getting wasted in the heat' line.[156]

My editor told me literary devices like this help you, the reader, get to know me, the author, better. I think the tidbit above keys you into the fact that my musical tastes haven't changed since high school and not much else. Still, I'll try and torture this prose to make the connections to the topic at hand: incentives.

Much like *Backstreets*, there are megahits in the world of management scholarship which have stood the test of time in terms of relevance and importance. One such article is *On the Folly of Rewarding A, While Hoping for B*[157] written by Steven Kerr[158] in 1975.[159] The article, which has been referenced by other academics thousands of times, famously claims,

> "*Whether dealing with monkeys, rats, or human*
> *beings, it is hardly controversial to state that*
> *most organisms seek information concerning*
> *what activities are rewarded, and then seek*

*to do (or at least pretend to do) those things, often to the virtual exclusion of activities not rewarded....Nevertheless, numerous examples exist of reward systems that are fouled up in that the types of behavior rewarded are those which the rewarder is trying to discourage, while the behavior desired is not being rewarded at all."*

Kerr provides numerous examples of this folly in business, government, medicine and consulting. One glaring example comes from sports, "Most coaches disdain to discuss individual accomplishments, preferring to speak of teamwork...however, rewards are distributed according to individual performance....The college basketball player who passes the ball to teammates instead of shooting will not compile impressive statistics and is less likely to be drafted by the pros. It therefore is rational for players to think of themselves first, and the team second."

Kerr sat for an interview celebrating the 40th anniversary of the article in 2015 and clarified a key insight, "What the 'Folly' is really about is that it is not always the employees' fault; management is responsible for all too many of the employee dysfunctionalities."[160] Or to borrow from Kerr's intellectual antecedent, B.F. Skinner,[161] don't blame the rat for its behavior.

Notwithstanding the terrible analogy between

employees and rats, what incentives does your organization currently reward? And are you consistently getting the right behaviors out of these incentives? A typical credit union has some sort of organizational scorecard with metrics that translate into a 'gain sharing'[162] scheme whereby employees across the organization receive a monetary award at the end of the year. These metrics are usually a combination of return on assets, capital ratio, customer satisfaction scores, lending growth and efficiency. You may be hitting the numbers but a closer analysis will likely reveal your organization is likely incentivizing the wrong type of behaviors. A great place to start this introspective look is through a good friend of mine[163] who has been working on this problem for the past few decades by creating a combination of open book management and self-funded incentive programs to ensure the right behaviors are being reinforced. Finally, I'd like to reinforce the importance of reading Kerr's classic management article due to its clarity and action-oriented approach. Plus, it is something you can bring up at your next cocktail party, "Have you read Kerr's 1975 paper on incentives ..."

## There Is Either Short-Term Pain Or Long-Term Pain

Have you ever taken a personality assessment? First time I did I was worried that it would come back negative.[164] In the various iterations of these assessments, I always get a readback that goes something like this, "George is a person who tends to relate to others by being tolerant, agreeable and accepting of others. He tends to avoid conflict and prefers instead to accommodate others' requests." This personality quirk leads to a few predictable outcomes in the work world: (a) in collaborative settings I thrive, (b) in competitive settings I fold like a cheap card table. Personality assessments tell a simplistic picture of one's tendencies, but early in my career I felt as if the die was cast and there was nothing I could do to change my personality.[165] As the years went on, I recognized that these assessments simply expressed how I prefer to act, and well sometimes you have to get out of your comfort zone to get shit done.

With apologies to the first people I directly managed in my career[166] I slowly discovered organizations cause all kinds of pain. There's your pain in the ass where you have to do a bunch of administrative stuff like expense reports and HR reporting. Then there's your pain in my head where you have to tap into big, strategic questions with no good answer, only uncertainty. Finally, there's your pain in the neck which comprises the catchall of aligning people around specific goals, fielding all manner of questions from co-workers such as "Why doesn't Brent use standard company software?, "Why does Josey get to leave at 3 pm everyday?" or "Why does Ben always wear pink shorts to work?"

Regardless of the ass, head or neck classification, there are always pains going on in any organization. You can't ignore these pains without experiencing massive downsides. As a person with an accommodating personality[167] I desperately want to ignore all these pains and assume everyone is a fully formed adult capable of figuring stuff out. But alas, there is either going to be short-term pain (better) or long-term pain (worse), so might as well swallow your personality and tackle things head on. Admittedly I have had a hard time doing this with people in my organization, but for some reason when I am brought in as an outside advisor, I don't have the same problem. For a few hours or a few days, I suspend my "come on people now, smile on each other, everybody get together try and love one another right now" personality and turn into a considerate, East Coast asshole. Maybe I act like this because these types of engagements are short-term in nature, but if my co-workers, friends or family members were to observe me in these settings they would readily call me an angry elf. Channel that courage to confront the various pains in your work world because you will either be uncomfortable in the short-term, or you'll let it play out and you'll still be uncomfortable but it will last a lot longer.

## The Value Of Sentimental Truisms And Homespun Wisdom

I'm the first to admit I cry. It's not that I'm super secure with my masculinity. It's that I simply get emotional with sentimental songs, stories and approaches. That Folgers ad where the kid comes home early from the Peace Corps and surprises her parents: weeping. Add to the list Foreigner's song *I Want to Know What Love Is* and most endings to formulaic romantic comedies. I know what's coming but it still gets me.

It's no surprise then that I've been attracted to sentimental truisms in the work world.

My first introduction to these truisms was as a counselor at Maryland Soccer School, which was created and run by legendary Washington, DC coaches, Dave "Scooter" Scaggs and Sam DeBone.[168] Scooter, as you can tell by his name, was a character of the first degree. Sam was the organized disciplinarian, but in retrospect probably the best coach I ever had. They created a conveyor belt of kids through his summer camp who then became counselors like me. The distinct thing about their approach was to have a model for a week of camp and replicate the hell out of that model. The schedule, still burned into my memory, went something like this every day:

Arrivals // All camp meeting // Skills Demonstration // Skills Training // Game // Lunch // Lecture // Watch Pele Movie // Skills Demonstration // Skills Training // All camp meeting // Departures

The lecture portion, which did not deviate from week to week or year to year, introduced me to a few sentimental truisms that resonate to this day:[169]

> *"Inch by Inch Life's a Cinch, Yard by Yard It's Very Hard"*

> *"You Can't Hoot with the Owls in the Evening and Soar with the Eagles in the Morning"*

> *"The Difference Between a Champ and a Chump is U (You)"*

At first glance (and second and third) these topics are simplistic, a bit silly... and kind of true. For example, if you want to succeed in life you have to take it slowly and methodically. Also, if you are out partying all the time you won't be at your best in the morning.[170] Finally, if you want to be a champion in something only you can control your destiny. Just reading this paragraph makes me feel like I'm about to sell you a time share or invite you into a multi-level marketing program (or coach you to play your best darn soccer game ever!!!). However, these sentimental approaches seem to work by creating a shortcut in your brain to your ultimate goal, whatever that may be.

As I aged out of the camp and entered the wide world of work I came across marginally more sophisticated sentimental truisms that have proven to be useful. So, would you like to take a look at three examples of these truisms? Of course you would!

Brag, Worry, Wonder, Bet is a nifty book[171] published in 2013 that guides managers on how to give feedback to their staff. The guidance is simple. When the manager provides feedback to a staffer, they first share what they 'brag' (strengths) about when talking about the employee. Next, they flip the script and share some of their 'worries' (weaknesses) about the staff member. Then, they provide a list of things they 'wonder' (opportunities) when they think about the employee. Finally, they end with a forward looking 'bet' on what the employee will accomplish over the next evaluation period. This approach is simple, achieves the aims of a feedback session and creates dialog rather than a complex, templated evaluation. The great thing about this truism is that you can apply the approach to all manner of management topics such as project and organizational evaluation. I've been known to use this line of questioning with board members at the beginning of strategic planning projects as a means to talk in real words (not business lingo) about their hopes, fears, confusions and views of the organization in the future.

My good friend, Rick Thomas, famously shared a bit of his homespun wisdom when we were Peace Corps Volunteers in the early 1990s in Uzbekistan. It went something like this, "If it's stupid but it works, it isn't stupid." I can't recall what Rick was referring to, but he has a practicality that is baked into all aspects of his life. Rick's sentiment captures the fact that we are all fakers, or put more generously, we live in a world of great uncertainty. Sure, people in all manner of professional settings have acquired varying levels of education, experience, skills and knowledge to help us do our jobs better. However, unless you are in a job with simple, repetitive tasks with very little external influence, the likelihood for success in projects, high-stakes decisions or strategy making is quite low. Rick, who has held an interesting array of jobs,[172] believes you just need to try things. If these things seem stupid at first, but work, let's listen to Rick and categorically state, "It isn't stupid". Rick does have a critical corollary to his truism: "You can't fix stupid". There is no get out of jail free card if you continue to do stupid things without positive results. According to Rick, you're just stupid!

Peter Drucker is regarded as one of the leading modern management thinkers.[173] He's most known for his 'management by objectives' approach, but what I've found most endearing about Drucker's work is the ease of access to his big mind. Here's his doozy of a quote to describe the pathology of most organizations, "Most of what we call management consists of making it difficult for people to get their work done". I can imagine Drucker stating this in his thick Austrian accent, providing a wry smile, dropping the mic and leaving the room. I'll end this chapter here because there is not much more to say about the topic of management other than to emphasize the fact that management is all about facilitating individual and collective success.

## Next Steps

Management is a broad field. If we are honest with ourselves, we've each likely had more failures than successes with managing people and projects. Context and timing matter. Personalities and goals combine to make things more complex. I can recall managing the same people in different contexts and projects with completely different outcomes. This chapter acknowledges the importance of management along with a few things I've seen work over the years. I believe there are general principles, not hard and fast rules, to consider as you continue your management journey from a human scale perspective. A few last thoughts that will likely be useful for anyone regardless of your managerial experience:

Better understand yourself by working within your organization or with a third- party expert to assess your personality type through a variety of publicly available tools. I would highly recommend The *Big Five Personality Test*[174] as a starting point.

Invest in professional development so that you gain exposure to a diversity of management approaches. Luckily, credit unions offer a host of opportunities for new and experienced managers, including Filene Research Institute, The Cooperative Trust, CUNA & Affiliates, NAFCU, state associations and, of course, Credit Union Executives Society (CUES)

Read <u>The Effective Executive</u> by Peter Drucker. It was published in 2006 and stands the test of time.

# CHAPTER 6

# STRATEGERY

*"Families is where our nation finds hope, where wings take dream."*

-George W. Bush

My wife is a master strategist. In all aspects of her life, she has a keen sense of the external environment. She knows her internal capabilities. And she is a determined goal setter who can concisely describe her desired future. I watch with awe how her strategic mind works. This set of circumstances has its downside: she's so damn competent that I rarely do much when she's around except reap the benefits of her expertise and skills.

I first experienced her strategist capabilities while we were in our initial courting phase as Peace Corps Volunteers in Uzbekistan. The external environment was such that we had very few rules to abide by,[175] so we decided to take advantage of the situation by going on a variety of non-sanctioned[176] trips around the country. She identified the right bus to take us to our destination, planned the appropriate type and amount of food to carry for the journey and developed a list of things we should see. I packed my own bag like a big boy, brought my sparkling personality and that's about it.

On one such trip, we traveled by bus (30 hours each

way) to the ancient Silk Road city of Samarkand. She made a huge batch of homemade hummus, picked up some flatbread, fruit and a few candy bars. The journey there was bumpy but just as anticipated. After a touch over 30 hours we rolled into the ancient city of Samarkand just as the sun was rising and walked to the accommodation she set up. The trip was memorable and left that knowing, very good feeling that we were likely going to be together for the rest of our lives.[177]

A few days later, as we were departing Samarkand from the dusty bus depot, an official looking guy (owing to his uniform) approached us and began asking friendly questions. This kind of situation was common during our 4-ish years in Uzbekistan as we looked very different from pretty much everyone else. Additionally, we spoke the local language, which immediately endeared us to nearly everyone we met.

However, the official's line of questioning quickly turned serious, leading us to believe that he wasn't super excited that a couple of Americans had learned his language and was interested in his culture. He quickly detained us for failing to register at the local immigration office.[178] His line of questioning veered from our bureaucratic failings to a more sinister set of inquiries. Our bags were searched, our papers were examined and our permission to even be in the country was questioned. In retrospect, this official was looking for a shakedown, which was fairly common at that point in the country's history, but at that moment I became nervous about the outcome of our detention. The official was keyed in to the fact that we had a dull knife in our bag and intimated that we could use it as a weapon to create an American hegemony in Central Asia.[179] The knife in question was an ornamental paring knife we used to crack open pomegranates, slice apples and re-enact the Indiana Jones bazaar scene.

Thinking he had us rattled, the official told us he was getting his supervisor and left us in his cramped office in the bus station. I was ready to admit our wrongdoings and commit to reeducation camps while my wife remained steely calm and composed. She looked up at the wall clock and said, "Our bus leaves in two minutes and the door is not locked. Let's just leave." The strategy she originally set forth (well-planned and seamless trip to Samarkand) was met with an external barrier (likely greedy but potentially scary official) so she assessed the situation, took stock of our capabilities and solved the problem. We gathered our things, scooted to the homeward bound bus and watched from our windows as Samarkand faded into the night. Midnight Express avoided!

Besides the fact that my wife is a kick-ass partner,

she embodies the strategic thinking skills that are the hallmark of any successful organization. Over the years I've worked with hundreds of individual credit union organizations on their strategies. This chapter sets forth an approach to strategy making that can help differentiate your organization and activate a more human approach to planning for the future.

## The Essence Of Strategy

I'm a Michael Porter fanboy. If Comic Con put on an offshoot convention for strategic thinkers, I'd totally cosplay Porter. I'd dye my hair gray, buy some tortoise shell glasses along with a tweed jacket and proclaim, "The essence of strategy is choosing what *not* to do" and "The essence of strategy is choosing to perform activities differently than rivals do." These two quotes come from Porter's seminal 1996 article entitled *What is Strategy*[180] and should form the basis for any organization's strategy. Sounds simple, but it's not.

For instance, at your next strategy meeting what if you were to ask your assembled luminaries two questions:

1. In the last 24 months what have we consciously stopped doing?
2. As an organization, what is the one thing we do so differently that normal people

talk about it?

For the first question, chances are your team of senior leaders would struggle to identify anything until an awkward amount of time elapses when someone slowly raises their hand and says, "Well, we finally got rid of travelers checks!" On the next question, you'd likely get a finessed answer that tortuously attempts to explain how your mortgage or checking product offers outstanding value compared to the bank down the street. With very few exceptions, most credit unions have a generic strategy without much thought put into trade-offs (e.g., when to say NO) and differentiation. As Porter pointed out when asked his verdict on the banking sector, "This industry is riddled with me-too competitors."[181]

Competition[182] in the retail banking sector has been on a slow boil the past few decades, but we are close to getting to the magical 212-degree Fahrenheit temperature where the boiling turns into roiling. Credit unions need to set their differentiated strategies now, especially considering the emerging competitive environment. Some topics to consider as early warning (weak) signals of large change:

Consolidation of banks and credit unions has been on a steady pace for decades.

Challenger banks and fintechs are moving up the value chain as predicted in the innovator's dilemma[183] (e.g., that market leaders are often set up to fail as industries are disrupted).

Consumers are used to (and expect) frictionless, contactless delivery of products and services, especially after forced behavior change during the pandemic.

Suppliers who furnish essential technology services are limiting your ability to meet emerging consumer needs because of long-term contractual agreements.

Regulation is a consistent hum that fluctuates with the policymakers in charge.

The long and short of Porter's teaching boils down to this: Stop piling more ornaments and tinsel on your "Christmas Tree".[184] Instead, think like a minimalist by choosing the things that truly differentiate your tree from other trees. How you go about this is informed by another thinker you should acquaint yourself with: Richard Rumelt.

## Good Strategy/Bad Strategy

Rumlet, a long tenured professor at UCLA, wrote a book[185] that is a mix of practice and practicality, which provides an implementation guide of sorts for Porter's advice. These two could very well be intellectual enemies or have some sort of consulting feud dating back to the 1980's, but I've found the combination of their work to be effective and extremely practical. Porter starts with the why; Rumelt comes in with the how.

First, let's start with Rumelt's easy pickings: bad strategy. He has a lot to say about the topic[186] and provides numerous cogent examples in one of his latest books, *Good Strategy Bad Strategy*. See if any of these bad strategy characteristics sound familiar to you:

*Lots of fluff and jargon in strategic planning documentation,*

*Fails to face up to or define the organization's key challenge,*

*Mistakes goals and metrics for strategy,*

*Long list of objectives that are not strategic.*

Rumelt then defines the hallmarks of a good strategy. Like Porter, he is parsimonious with his guiding principles. Good strategy contains just three key elements:

*A good diagnosis of the problem the organization is trying to solve for,*

*A guiding policy for fixing this problem ,*

*A coherent set of actions to put the policy into place.*

Summarizing Porter and Rumelt's greatest hits you can easily assess your current strategy by asking yourself 5 questions:

1. In our strategy-making process do we frequently say "no" to ideas?
2. Is our strategy different from our competitors?
3. What problem are we trying to solve with our strategy?
4. What policies do we have in place to solve these problems?
5. What coherent actions do we conduct to enforce these policies?

Sounds simple, but it's not. Each question contains pitfalls and difficult decisions that invariably lead to conflict inside the boardroom, amongst your staff and amongst other stakeholders. Meditate on these five questions because they represent the critical components of a good (or bad) strategy. The next few sections will discuss creative strategic add-ons—consider them in conjunction with the above five points.

## The Love-Hate Paradox

If you graduated from a university, chances are you had a rival institution that you absolutely hate. As previously mentioned, I'm a proud (double) graduate of University of Wisconsin-Madison. I originally ended up there on a soccer scholarship where I played four years and managed to have a higher GPA than my seasonal goal tally.[187] If you are a fellow Badger, you likely hold deep animosity towards Michigan first with Ohio State being a close second. As an athlete in what are lovingly called 'non-revenue sports,' my rivalries were different. Indiana University, another Big Ten school, was the nation's soccer powerhouse for decades. The Hooisers carried an air about them that was arrogant. What made it even more frustrating was that they were so damn good. By the time my senior year came around we had lost every time we played them...in the HISTORY of our program. In my senior year we turned the tables on them in an early fall match and beat them in a 1-0 thriller. Unfortunately, we also faced them in the Big Ten tournament final and lost. And lost again, in double overtime, in the NCAA tournament, my last meaningful game as a soccer player if you don't count the highly competitive over 50 league I still participate in on Thursday nights in Middleton, Wisconsin. This final game played in Bloomington, Indiana was attended by a few hundred traveling fans from Madison.

The night before the match a few of these individuals snuck onto the Hooiser's beautiful soccer specific pitch and spray painted "UW Soccer " on the center mark. So, while we left Indiana disappointed we knew we had, literally, left our mark. To this day, I can't hold my tongue when someone mentions Indiana University as there is a hate that is so deep and visceral. On the other hand, there is a love that is so deep for the Badgers.

In the course of your strategy making, can you create elements of this love-hate paradox? Most credit unions try to stay in the 'pregnant middle' by positioning themselves as either friendly, convenient, value-oriented, or a combination of all three. This milquetoast approach doesn't tap into the human connections people crave and threatens to push your brand to the back of consumers' minds.[188]

Your love-hate paradox doesn't have to be the central portion of your strategy like the Cooperative Bank example we discussed earlier. Rather, this paradox can be in how you serve your customers. For example, a handful of large credit unions[189] eschew face-to-face delivery channels in favor of digital and other remote delivery choices. Some consumers love this approach. Some consumers hate this approach. But there are very few consumers who would not have an opinion on this approach. This is where the paradox comes in. For those that love something they REALLY love it, use it widely and tell their friends, family and co-workers. The opposite is true for those who REALLY hate the approach and don't use it widely so they don't tell their friends, family or co-workers.

## Deep Vertical Focus And Narrow Sphere

My children are at the age when they actually ask for advice. Recently I felt I gave Huck, my elder, really bad advice on his career. I told him to follow his passions and good things will come. Upon further reflection, and after avidly listening to the Prof G podcast,[190] the advice should have been, "Be really good at something very specific and hone that skill for years and years until you are an expert." Passion is reserved for people who have the means to focus on non-pecuniary[191] careers, have received a calling from a higher power[192], or got really lucky following their passion, got rich and now encourage others to similarly follow their passion.

This advice is good for someone's career and your organization's focus. Every credit union got their start being a provider of limited services to a narrow selection of the population, likely through an employer or another associational relationship. Of course times change[193] and your focus needs to change with the times, but the days of (trying) to be all things to all people should be in the rearview mirror. Instead identify a target market that is large enough to support your economic model and go very deep with that group. Credit unions focused on teachers and universities provide an enlightening example of how this deep/narrow focus works in contemporary society.

My primary credit union, University of Wisconsin Credit Union (UWCU), was chartered in 1931 to serve the needs of the faculty and staff of the University of Wisconsin-Madison. For many years the focus stayed on the needs of this small, but powerful group of individuals. Only in the relatively recent past did UWCU begin to focus on the needs of students at their flagship institution. Still pretty narrow despite having a student body of about 40,000 people. Fast forward to the present, and UWCU serves the financial needs of the 13 UW System satellite campuses and their 165,000 students, the nearly one million alumni from these institutions across the globe and, most recently, pretty much anyone of the 5.8 million residents of Wisconsin.

While the potential reach of UWCU is quite large, their universe of expertise is still very narrow and centered around University life: debit accounts, student loans, home loans, car loans and investment accounts are their bread and butter. If you want a commercial services account, UWCU is not going to be able to serve you. They chose to say "No" to this segment of the population.

For those institutions without the storied history of a Big Ten university, more creative approaches must be instituted. For instance, most original airline credit unions no longer rely on a single sponsor relationship (e.g., airline employees). Institutions like American Airlines FCU have identified airline-adjacent opportunities —contractors that work at airports—as an emerging market for their product set. Alliant, the former United Airlines Employees CU, serves employees of other large corporations around the US with a mobile workforce including Google and UnitedHealthCare.

By focusing on narrow interests, your organization has the potential to better tap into the affinity and affiliative needs of consumers which have been diminishing for several decades.[194] It is aspirational to think credit unions can fill that void, but as actress Lily Tomlin famously said, "I said 'Somebody should do something about that.' Then I realized I am somebody." Credit unions are that 'Somebody'.

## Your Positioning Statement Is The Bulwark Of Strategic Differentiation

During my first few weeks at Filene I asked a neighbor for some advice on marketing. Since its founding 1989, Filene had been a resource for credit unions, but never marketed itself. As a result, we had a core group of supporters but low awareness across the industry. This neighbor runs an extremely successful marketing agency[195] with major national client brands and decades of experience. Since Filene couldn't afford his professional services, I bought him a cup of coffee and simply listened. It was like sitting at the feet of a guru.

His core message: "Our process is simple: simplify, then amplify."

I wanted to reply, "But teacher, how might one simplify and then amplify?" But he was busy billing corporate clients so he couldn't really elaborate too much. I reflected on his pronouncement and placed it in the context of strategy. Once you've gone through the strategy process, you come to a certain truth about your brand and offerings. For the end user this truth is the hard work you do in the strategy process to simplify the thousands or millions of things you do into a pithy positioning statement. In other words, 'Here's why you should choose me over the other brand.' Once you understand your simple truth you have to amplify that truth over and over again to customers, potential customers, the community, employees, board, and policymakers. And, then you have to amplify the truth again so that it becomes a shortcut in your members' (or potential members') brains.

This approach to positioning, like most of the topics in this chapter, seems simple on the surface but is so hard to execute. I can back this assertion up through direct experience with hundreds of credit union planning experiences. For quite a few credit unions, I would ask planning participants to read a 1 ½ page article (which they loved) called "Strategize on a Napkin."[196] Then I would ask them to draw a picture of their credit union's strategy on a napkin (which they hated) so that a normal consumer would be activated to join the credit union.

When planning day came, I'd invite board members and senior executives to present their masterpiece as an icebreaker for the session. Across organizations, the level of creativity and artistry was strong and affirmed the importance of a humanities education; however, within most of these organizations strategic consistency was missing. With very few exceptions, each person had a different view of the organization's strategy.

They hadn't done the work of simplifying all the stuff they do into a central truth, and they certainly hadn't amplified that truth across the organization. This is not meant as a castigation, but simply an observation.

I went through this exercise for the creation of my firm: Hofheimer Strategy Advisors. As a sole proprietorship I didn't have to worry too much about alignment of my staff or board, so instead I sought counsel and insights from a collection of work, family and personal contacts. I asked this group a simple question, "How would you describe my unique ability?" Ninety-nine percent of the respondents took this assignment seriously while a few dorks from my college days replied with quips such as, "great eyes" and "wonderful dancer". The useful responses[197] helped to home in on the truth about my unique ability, which I then amplified into the following positioning statement: "Advising highly ambitious credit unions that want to change the world." While far from perfect this statement does a lot in a few words, and in your strategy making process you should aspire for something similar. Since credit unions are focused on the needs of humans, your statement needs to focus on their needs and stay away from what Rumelt calls fluff and jargon.

The best strategic positioning statement I've seen for a credit union is Self-Help Credit Union's

"Economic Opportunity for All." They back up this statement with unique products, historical proof points, and a host of activities that make it hard to classify them as simply a credit union. Study their approach[198] and I guarantee you will learn something you can apply to your own institution.

On a slightly more off-the-cuff approach, look to a mentor (and co-worker) of mine, Franck Schuurmans, who was an advisor to credit unions and other large corporate clients before his untimely passing in 2015. Franck claimed credit unions were spending too much time and money on things that didn't matter to people. Through his experience and practical/ thrifty Dutch upbringing he advocated for credit unions to buy full page ads in *USA Today*[199] simply stating, "Credit Unions: You Won't Get Screwed!". Simple and true. Should that be amplified?

## One Of Three Strategic Outcomes

One of the very first people I met in credit unions was a gent named John Oliver. Not THAT John Oliver, however he is also from England, emigrated to the United States and has a sharp wit that will keep you rolling during a long enjoyable dinner. John works with boards of credit unions and banks across the world and once he gets into these boardrooms he turns into an admitted cranky old man. John often jokes with me that clients love having a beverage of choice with him before the engagement because of his delightful British demeanor, but once he gets them in the decision-making process they can't stand him. John will further joke that is just fine by him because he can't understand why anyone would want to socialize with him in the first place.

The basis for most of John's crankiness comes from his common pronouncements that credit unions (and banks) can have one of three strategic outcomes: bigger, better, <u>or</u> different. He gives no quarter to those that claim to focus on all three. To which John replies, "Sorry. You have to choose one. Strategy is hard. Stiff upper lip. Pip pip cheerio." I think he's right.

Credit unions tend to have a list of organizational metrics that are usually presented in a scorecard approach[200] that captures all the things that are important to the organization. This type of approach is important, however, there are some things that are more important than others. So, try to channel John's bigger, better *or* different choice set and emphasize the one most important outcome measurement for your success.

## Scale Is Elusive

Scale is one of those words that doesn't make sense unless you understand the context. A CEO could state, "My organization needs scale in order to serve our community better."

If you are not versed in this usage you'd wonder why (a) the CEO didn't put an article (most likely "the") before the word scale[201] or (b) what the heck does a credit union need to weigh before it serves its community.

Scale in this context roughly means a balance sheet big enough to efficiently amortize all the costs necessary to be a high-performing organization. Previously we talked about the various (and increasing) demands put on credit unions from outside sources such as consumer needs/wants, technological innovations, regulatory pressures, competitor moves, etc. Logically, the scale argument makes sense. If you only have a $100 million balance sheet and you have to make the same investments as an organization with a $1 billion balance sheet, the latter is likely going to have a lower per dollar asset cost than the former.

A 2020 report by the FDIC[202] provides a nuanced view of the community banking sector's scale circumstances. They state, " We find evidence that almost all gains from increased size accrue early in the size distribution: by approximately $300 million in loan portfolio size, banks have achieved about 90 percent of the potential efficiencies estimated to occur by increasing in size from $10 million to $3.3 billion; by $600 million, they have achieved about 95 percent of potential efficiencies." Pretty astounding that 90% of a community financial institution's scale is achieved at the $300 million loan portfolio size. Once you creep up in size, economies of scale make only marginal contributions.

I share this information because I've worked with many credit unions that have a stated asset target for the sole purpose of gaining economies of scale —regardless of their size. There is little awareness of the reality uncovered by the FDIC.

I once had an interesting back-to-back illustration of this. First, I worked with a credit union in rural North Carolina that wanted to crest the $100 million in assets category so as to achieve economies of scale. The next day I zipped over to California to work with another institution that was striving for the $10 billion in assets category for the same reason. The point is that scale is elusive and likely accruing benefits at the lower rather than higher end of size market. Growing from one billion to two billion in assets isn't likely to change your cost structure, but moving from 200 million to 300 million may. Rather than trying to grow your way out of the scale equation, go back to the original strategy tenets and decide what you are going to say "no" to. Chances are your organization's cost structure will improve by making difficult decisions to eliminate or decrease a portion of your business that holds little to no value. Growth will be a nice outcome, but it shouldn't be the goal.

## There Is No One Right Way/Model For Success

My first real job was with Price Waterhouse that was once deemed one of the big six consulting firms. The experience was beneficial but not enjoyable. I jumped through the ranks quite quickly (and luckily) because I was in the right place at the right time. As a result, I got to interact with a host of characters that provided direct consulting services to clients and the partners that lorded over them. Over the course of several years I observed a lot of things. First, I knew I didn't want to stay in this field because the end game is becoming a partner and almost all the partners were divorced, overweight and/or struggling with some sort of psychological crisis that was self-medicated through way too much alcohol. I also learned the craft of 1990s consulting and its associated lingo. I've waxed on (and off) about my distaste for this figure of language, and here are a few that really grind my gears:

> *"We are not here to boil the ocean"* ... a pithy statement to say that's a lot of work and I don't think I want to do all that work.

*"That's out of scope"* … a passive aggressive way to tell the client if you want me to do that, we have to write up another scope of work order, and it's going to cost you more money.

*"Now that I have a better idea of the questions"* … at the end of a project when you don't give the client what they want, but you discover something else you can bill them for.

I will make one exception for shmarmy 'consulting-speak' because (a) the phrase is rarely used and (b) it doesn't involve a consultant trying to sell more services to a client: "there's no such thing as a silver bullet, but there is such a thing as a silver buckshot." **This point speaks to the human nature of credit unions' success: a multitude of scientific, behavioral, operational and strategic factors determine whether you are going to be successful, or not. This point speaks to the human nature of credit unions' success: a multitude of scientific, behavioral, operational and strategic factors determine whether you are going to be effective or not.**

Remember Porter's exhortation that financial services is filled with "me-too" competition? Well, that's because the entire industry is endlessly benchmarking itself against other competitors that look and act like them. Executives are rewarded for achieving a certain level of percentile performance in a multitude of benchmarks. If an executive falls behind on their scores, they ask consultants to share what others are doing to achieve those benchmarks to which the consultants happily regurgitate plans from another client.

The feeling is, "If it's good enough for X, then it's good enough for us."

I propose a different approach. One that acknowledges the context in which one organization operates may be similar to others, but also considers the previously mentioned factors to create a truly unique situation. Yes, it is important to look at case studies of highly effective organizations, but their way is not your way, grasshopper. The silver bullet of trying to copy competitors has played out in a variety of industries[203] with limited success. The silver buckshot approach recognizes your credit union has its own insights, equipment and talents that don't quite match what others recommend. There is no one right way to success and the successful find their own way.

## Some Acronyms Are Okay

As you can tell I'm not big on generic advice or acronyms, but I'm going to make an exception for corporate social responsibility (CSR) and environmental, social and governance (ESG).

These two items should be high on the list for most credit union strategy conversations. Some in the industry refer to this topic under the 'social impact' banner.

CSR is best defined by David Blood[204] as, "the explicit recognition that social, economic, environmental, and ethical factors directly affect business strategy." Similarly, ESG is an emergent trend encouraging (and in some jurisdictions requiring) organizations to report out to key stakeholders their impact on society and the environment along with detailed governance practices. Simply look up standards-setting organizations like Global Reporting Initiative and B-Corps to acquaint yourselves with what this new environment may look like. Or you can look closer to home with voluntary reports being issued by credit unions of all shapes and sizes.[205]

This interest in the intersection of society and business is not new. In 1926 Edward A. Filene, the father of U.S. credit unions, stated in his book *A Way Forward*, "I think I can truly say that I have always dealt with matters of social justice, cooperation and general welfare, not on the basis of philanthropy or paternalism, but as essential factors in the development of successful business."

What is new is the increasing scrutiny being put on organizations' behavior.

The evidence is becoming clearer that organizations with a strong CSR profile and effective ESG practices gain the following advantages:

*Positive word of mouth, increased patronage and stronger brand loyalty,[206]*

*Reputational advantages over others in your industry, [207]*

*Advantages in talent acquisition and retention, [208]*

*Ability to charge premium prices over competitors, [209]*

*Existence of a positive "halo effect" around non-CSR activities within the organization.[210]*

Ok, so being 'prosocial' seems to link with good organizational outcomes, but is it causal or correlative? Dunno, but here's something to consider: As the world around us changes and more attention is paid to business' role in society, consumers are expecting you to do more than return economic value to stakeholders.

Additionally, regulators around the world are creating frameworks for required reporting on

ESG factors.[211] These regulatory requirements usually start in Europe, flow down to publicly traded companies and then work their way into weirdos like credit unions. I have no idea as to the timeline of these events, but as my favorite scientist Louis Pasteur once said, "Chance only favors the prepared mind."

Plus, credit unions are uniquely positioned to own the prosocial mantle in financial services... wouldn't it be a shame if Wells Fargo got ahead of credit unions on social impact simply because they were forced to by their regulators or just because they have a bigger marketing megaphone?

Research by Filene[212] illustrated credit unions are in the middle of the CSR (or prosocial or ESG or social impact) pack. Many credit unions boil down the concept of CSR to a timid, tactical and ancillary activity. Flip through the pages of any credit union system or credit union league newsletter and it's not long before you find it: the shot of a big check shot held aloft by smiling credit union employees and the check's grateful recipient. These shots are both heartwarming and discouraging. Sure, those checks are visible proof credit unions are hard at work being responsible corporate citizens. But they also illustrate something else: many credit unions may be missing an opportunity for greater impact and leverage.

If transported to present-day, how would Ed Filene grade today's credit unions? Without a doubt, he would marvel at our large, growing and financially healthy balance sheet. More than $2 trillion would be unimaginable to him. However, if you believe (like Filene did) that there is something more to credit unions besides buying money through deposits, selling money through loans and managing the margins, then our founders may have a few critical questions. Ed, short in stature but a giant analytical mind, would cross-examine you on the specific, quantifiable activities you are undertaking with your annual profits. These same assessments have been, and will continue to be, asked by your members, policymakers and boards of directors.

What follows is an industry-wide proposal to prepare your credit union for these growing entreaties around social impact. It's a big ask but why not go to the edge, and then bring it back to reality.[213]

## A New Approach: The Credit Union Tithe

I propose each credit union commit to allocating 10% of budgeted (or actual) net earnings to authentic social impact activities on an annual basis. Similar to tithing in religious practice, I believe this approach is feasible and beneficial for a number of reasons:

*Simplifies a Core Credit Union Function.*
The old maxim, "What gets measured gets done" can be modified slightly to, "What gets budgeted gets done". A 10% allocation of net earnings provides a concise and clear budget for CSR activities that everyone from the board chair to the frontline representative can understand and communicate.[214] Additionally, the fund ebbs and flows with economic conditions: in good times like 2009 to the present the amounts are massive; 2007-2008, not so much.

*Enables Collaboration on an Institution and Industry Level.*
Credit unions love to talk about being part of a cooperative movement. One of the cleverest retorts to this statement is, "Our cooperative movement rarely cooperates, and it doesn't move very much."[215] Only a true cynic would hold this statement as fact; however, there is a bit of truth to it. Credit unions (particularly those in the U.S.) find large scale collaboration difficult due to the number and variety of institutions. This approach scales an activity that recognizes the diversity of each institution's capability, is easy to implement and taken collectively can impart real impact.

*Identifies Differentiation Measures Beyond Pricing.*
Traditionally credit unions point to their

pricing advantage as one of their key strategic differentiators. The data supports this assertion with CUNA & Affiliates estimating a $10.2 billion annual benefit to consumers in the form of higher yields of savings, lower interest rates on loans and fewer/lower fees. This big number is a very rational representation of the credit union difference. However, consumers are also activated by non-economic[216] measures, including activities around a firm's social responsibility initiatives. What is missing is a standard measure of impact across the industry that will move consumers and policymakers. If every credit union were to have taken the 10% pledge in 2019, $1.48 Billion would have been allocated to social impact initiatives. That would have been the largest philanthropic gift of any commercial organization in the United States.

*Passes the Financial Sustainability Test.*
How would an annual $1.48 Billion in community investments impact the bottom line? The math is pretty straight-forward: 10% of earnings would simply reduce the credit union system's net income by 10% per year. Collectively from 1979-2016 this figure would equal $14.205B. If we were to assume (a) no change to the asset mix over this time frame, (b) no impact to profitability over this time frame, and (c) no impact to asset or membership growth over this time frame, the credit union system's net worth ratio would stand

at a healthy 9.79% vs. the actual ratio of 10.9%. But I think we can safely assume this $14 billion investment would create a positive net benefit to credit unions, right?

*Provides a Strong Tool for Public Policy Discourse.*
The U.S. credit union income tax exemption is an important public policy tool and judging by its longevity and bi-lateral support this policy is likely to stay on the books for some time.[217] Industry advocates work tirelessly to illustrate the benefit of this tax exemption to policy makers and consumers alike. The credit union tithe could be another proof point of the credit union difference. In addition to the massive pricing benefits credit unions confer on their members, a 10% voluntary give for social impact initiatives would likely be viewed favorably from a policy perspective. For comparative purposes, financial services firms paid an effective corporate tax rate of just 20.8% in 2016.[218]

*Brings Credit Unions into the CSR Conversation.*
Just over a decade ago, my cosplay buddy Michael Porter presciently concluded, "CSR can be much more than just a cost, constraint or charitable deed. Approached strategically, it generates opportunity, innovation, and competitive advantage for corporations – while solving pressing societal problems."

Ed Filene would likely nod his head and ask business leaders, "What took you so long to figure that chestnut out?" CSR is here to stay; to wit, "In successive polls, run by the Economist Intelligence Unit (EIU) and others, the percentage of managers regarding CSR as a high priority has been steadily increasing."[219] Additionally, the number of public and private companies that voluntarily report sustainability initiatives to the Global Reporting Initiative has skyrocketed from 12 in 1999 to over 14,000 today.[220]

## Next Steps

Like a bit of a jazz interlude, my hope with this last bit was to give you a sense of how strategy can come together at credit unions. I'm passionate about the ESG opportunity for credit unions and the past few pages represent hundreds of hours of reading, thinking and contemplating a strategy that would hopefully make Ed Filene proud. We all love frameworks and templates, but those approaches mask the fact that strategy is fundamentally about humans taking stock of a situation, making assumptions, deciding on things and, here's where the magic happens, building something different and useful. So, here are some useful suggestions to keep strategy making a human scale activity within your organization:

Read everything Michael Porter has to say about strategy, a good place to start is the Institute for Strategy and Competitiveness at Harvard Business School.[221]

Read the book <u>Good Strategy/Bad Strategy</u> by Richard Rumelt.

Ensure your organization's strategic discussions are consistently held throughout the organization, and not confined to a weekend retreat with only the board of directors and senior management in attendance.

Bone up on all things ESG through such sources as Ceres[222] (environmental), GABV[223] (social) and John Oliver, the grumpy Brit[224] (governance) to prepare for the future.

# CHAPTER 7

# THE END OF THE BEGINNING.

*Now this is not the end. It is not even the beginning of the end. But it is, perhaps, the end of the beginning.*
                                        *- Winston Churchill*

Since Milo, my youngest child, was a wee one, they hated team sports despite the fact that they were athletically gifted. I recall when Milo was just over 2 years old, they got on a two wheeled bike and just went. No training wheels, just go! As their proud papa, I followed Milo excitedly on foot around our neighborhood as they zoomed up and down our street. As their confidence grew, they went further afield and I found it harder and harder to keep up with Milo's pumping legs. One early spring day, Milo decided to head down to the concrete pier jutting out into Madison's Lake Mendota. Unaccustomed to a road ending, Milo kept pumping and accelerating their bike without a care, thinking it funny as I doggedly trailed behind, unable to catch up or warn them of the impending launch into the icy lake. In the front of my mind flashed images of Carrie not being pleased with my fathering skills. Milo didn't have a sudden epiphany about space and time logic, instead they hurtled into the lake. Amazingly, Milo didn't get hurt despite the five-foot drop into a partially frozen Lake Mendota. Milo cried, quickly recovered and got back on their bike to pedal home and tell Mom about the adventure. I coached Milo a bit on the details.

Today Milo is a dancer. They are graceful. They are creative. Milo is also gender fluid. They are the perfect distillation of the need for human-scale thinking. Many people, myself included, have a hard time understanding how gender identity falls on a spectrum rather than as a binary notion. I've made mistakes on Milo's pronouns, tried, with varying degrees of effectiveness, to understand their perspectives **and** unequivocally support their journey. What is shocking is the level of hateful rhetoric and lack of empathy in some corners to not even engage in understanding humans like Milo. Politicians and others fan the flames on this (and an increasing number of topics), but it strikes me how many people are simply missing out with their closed minds and lack of imagination. I feel sorry for these individuals because they are missing out on a rich world of creativity and opportunity.

I wrote this book to explore the thesis that in a world dominated by rigid concepts like scale and technology, there is an opportunity to operate on a more human scale. We are missing opportunities when we view the world as black **or** white rather than shades of gray. I've tried to present what this human-centered approach looks like in a variety of contexts specifically for people in the credit union industry. By applying these concepts inside and outside the business world, I can't help but imagine a renewed (and more positive) view of how we all interact and live alongside each other. Oh, and be on the lookout for Milo, they are going places.

## Putting Human Scale To The Test

In the Spring of 2021, I got a chance to test out this human scale perspective by pedaling my bike from San Diego, California to Saint Augustine, Florida. The plan was to travel over 3,000 miles solo, self-supported with my trusty steel bike, minimal clothes[225] and camping gear. For the first week of the journey, I was a lone soul endlessly rotating my pedals up and down mountains in Southern California and into the desert Southwest. It was fun, but the human connection was missing. Sure, I had the occasional interaction with people on the road,[226] but mostly it was me having conversations with me, myself and I.

About ten days into the journey, I arrived at a janky RV park in Globe, Arizona to set up for the night. $10 got me a shower and washing machines as well as a place to set up my luxurious 1-person tent. I decided to head into town for some grub. When I returned to the campsite, I saw four other smelly bikers setting up camp. This was the genesis of a group of eight[227] (and sometimes 12[228]) people who pedaled across the continent over the next five weeks. We ranged in age from early 20s to mid-70s and we learned so much from each other.

There was the occasional conflict, but mostly the ITC[229] was a bizarre (and farty) machine that somehow ended up dipping our bike tires in the Atlantic Ocean all in one piece. Along the adventure our mass of humanity sometimes resembled Forrest Gump and his band of followers. We would descend on some rural gas station in Texas or Louisiana and the conversations began very quickly. Sure we met some weirdos like the guy in the Hill Country of Texas who ran us off the road in his pickup truck—to this day I'm convinced he was actor Gary Busey. But, overwhelmingly, we encountered people who were naturally curious about us and us about them. We were invited into countless homes, provided free drinks/food and engaged in the most interesting conversations.

This experience was made richer because of human interaction and also the contrarian way of seeing the United States. A slow roll of 12 miles per hour for six weeks was a temporary cure for technology's incessant pinging, the overriding characteristic of today's society. I was forced to slow down, recognize my surroundings, observe the change of seasons/landscape and genuinely interact with people without much of a deadline. Not everyone will have this kind of luxury of time and space, but there are micro moments of opportunity to think, feel and operate on a human scale[230].

I'm under no illusion that the world hasn't changed dramatically in recent decades, but by consciously channeling human scaled approaches to consumer interactions, research, innovation, management and strategy, credit unions can thrive in this competitive landscape.

## Amplifying Ed's Genius

After Edward A. Filene's death in 1937, a consortium of his former colleagues published a book of his speeches entitled *Speaking of Change*[231]. In the book's introduction, the editors published an essay entitled "Ain't No Such Person," which memorialized Filene's vision and accomplishments. One section of this essay hits on the principles FIlene was fighting for in the 1930s that are eerily similar to the ones we're examining today:

> *More than a quarter of a century ago ...*
> *Edward A. Filene reached the conclusion that*
> *American finance must be democratized, but*
> *nobody knew what he meant. People either*
> *had money or they didn't; and if they had*
> *more than they cared to spend they loaned it*
> *out at interest, on well-recognized security,*

*thus accumulating still more money. That, as everybody understood, was finance. One might feel sorry for those who had no money, but what could anybody do about it? And how could such cruel facts be democratized?*

*Filene didn't feel sorry. Nevertheless, he founded the Credit Union movement in the United States; and in the credit unions, people who had almost no money and needed loans desperately, began to save their small sums collectively and to borrow from their collective selves and to pay interest to themselves on all the sums they borrowed. They had no security which the bank would recognize as security, and the laws of the various states did not recognize their unions as banks. But the experiment worked.*

*All that was necessary, it seemed, was to change the banking laws of all the states and of the nation, and make the masses acquainted with this type of co-operative credit, and then we would have a real object lesson in the democratization of finance.*

*This has cost Edward A. Filene, all told,
something over a million dollars, for which
he has never either sought or received a
penny in return. But don't imagine that
there was anything philanthropic about it;
for Filene is a selfish businessman, who just
happened to notice sooner than most that
the prosperity of every business depended
upon the prosperity of all legitimate
business, and that the prosperity of all
business depended upon adequate financing
of the masses who directly or indirectly make
its markets.*

*In the winter of 1932-33, before the nation
had got over its first thrill of the New Deal,
Filene made an extensive tour of America.
In city after city, to his utter amazement,
he was given the sort of ovation usually
reserved for presidents or presidential
candidates. It was a spontaneous ovation
on the part of thousands of adoring credit
unionists. For the laws of thirty-eight states
and the District of Columbia had now
recognized the credit unions as legitimate
banks; and although thousands of banks*

*all over America had closed their doors, the credit unions had uniformly weathered the depression, and credit unionism was experiencing its greatest era of expansion. But Edward A. Filene, instead of pausing for congratulations, is goading all concerned to renewed efforts to meet the rapidly changing economic conditions, and warning the credit unions of the necessity of the "next step forward".*

## The Next Step Forward

For me, the next step forward will be involve advising highly ambitious credit unions who want to change the world. Since late 2020, I've worked with 40 such ambitious organizations on 60 unique projects applying the concepts and ideas presented in this book with some impressive outcomes. However, much like my recent cross-country biking experience, I've found something was missing as a solo operator. It's a lonely existence hanging out at the Hampton Inn by yourself on Wednesday night somewhere in America. Plus one's capabilities and ideas become stale with just one person.

So in 2023, my former colleague from Filene, Brent Dixon, and I will be launching a venture called

The Strategy Cooperative at www.strategy.coop. Brent and I will continue to advise highly ambitious credit unions with the explicit purpose of "keeping the credit union movement moving". We aim to help solve myriad problems facing credit unions through a variety of human scale offerings. For instance, we will make the strategy making process more inclusive through a toolset which gathers and evaluates diverse stakeholder opinions across the credit union. Additionally, we will facilitate formal peer networking groups inside credit unions to ensure everyone "gets" the strategy and contributes towards their organization's long-term ambitions. We will also create simple yet insightful assessments that enable credit unions to do a quick check up on all manner of their organization's priorities. We have a bunch of other stuff up our sleeve with the express intent of helping credit unions win in a world dominated by scale and technology. Or, in short, making banking more human.

I hope you can join me on this journey.

---

[1] $4.00 for a case of beer, after returning the bottles in suitable shape.

[2] Except Alex P. Keaton

[3] I was not a mathlete

[4] https://s3.amazonaws.com/cfsi-innovation-files-2018/wp-content/uploads/2020/10/26135655/2020PulseTrendsReport-

Final-1016201.pdf

[5]      https://www.federalreserve.gov/publications/2020-economic-well-being-of-us-households-in-2019-dealing-with-unexpected-expenses.htm

[6]      See      Opportunity      Insights      (https://opportunityinsights.org/) for a deep dive on this topic and other astounding economic analyses.

[7] Even today the collective assets of credit unions would put them at the 5th largest banking institutions in the U.S. behind JPMorgan Chase, Bank of America, Wells Fargo and Citibank.

[8] The credit union industry's think and do tank.

[9] Any person or organization with even a mild interest in credit unions should join Filene Research Institute immediately!

[10] Filene kept finding the same characteristics so we stopped doing this research.

[11]      https://www.cunamutual.com/-/media/cunamutual/about-us/credit-union-trends/public/cutr_2022_10.pdf

[12] It should be noted that I was born in 1970 and that is the year the decline in community financial institutions commenced. Cause or correlation?

[13]      https://www.dupaco.com/about/what-is-dupaco/our-history/

[14] $i^3$ is a collection of next generation credit union leaders and one of the best professional development programs available to credit unions.

[15] An extremely visual non-sequitur that requires the reader to think deeply how a fart might travel over a hot skillet.

[16] The $i^3$ program is responsible for a variety of innovations in the market today: Savvy Money, Save to Win, and Savings Revolution to name a few.

[17]      https://www.cdc.gov/nchs/products/visual-gallery/obesity.htm?Sort=Title%3A%3Aasc

[18] Though the jury is still out on me.

[19] https://www.fuqua.duke.edu/faculty/dan-ariely

[20] https://filene.org/learn-something/reports/why-chose-a-credit-union-an-ethnographic-study-of-member-behaviors

[21] Do this in person, not electronically.

[22] https://filene.org/learn-something/reports/effective_managers

[23] https://www.fastcompany.com/54246/listener-runner-intuit

[24] Credit unions' long running customer service advantages are being challenged by commercial banks. (find source on Customer Satisfaction)

[25] You are likely seeing a pattern of talking to actual human beings in the creation of your organization's tactics and strategies.

[26] http://www.ushotelappraisals.com/

[27] This example borrows from a case study France Frei wrote about Commerce Bank's service model, https://www.hbs.edu/faculty/Pages/item.aspx?num=29457

[28] https://www.huffpost.com/entry/starbucks_n_4890735

[29] Triple, Venti, Half Sweet, Non-Fat, Caramel Macchiato

[30] Cobra Kai: Strike First, Strike Hard, No Mercy

[31] In truth, this product is a re-tread of 'at work' loans regularly offered at employer-sponsored credit unions from the 'olden days'.

[32] Rhino Foods makes, among other things, the cookie dough that goes into Ben & Jerry's (and most other brands) ice cream. All praise Rhino Foods!

[33] Rhino Foods created a foundation to encourage businesses to implement this concept which they call Income Advance. A full implementation guide can be found at https://www.rhinofoodsfoundation.org/

[34] See Silicon Valley Bank

[35] I'm looking at you Andrew Downin and Tansley Stearns

[36] https://web.archive.org/web/20200906015619/https://www.co-operativebank.co.uk/assets/pdf/bank/aboutus/ethicalpolicy/ethical-policy.pdf

[37] In later years they added such topics as landmine manufacturing, environmental degradation, labor rights, transfer of arms to oppressive regimes and climate change to name a few.

[38] You can see a selection of these videos at https://www.youtube.com/user/CooperativeBank/featured

[39] https://www.youtube.com/watch?v=J3xdq5miyfE

[40] Chris runs a very entertaining and informative podcast series which can be found at https://cfcfe.eu/audio/

[41] Regrettably the Cooperative Bank fell on hard times due to well documented governance and management failures which was well documented by the so-called "Kelly Review" at https://www.co-operative.coop/investors/kelly-review

[42] https://www.afi.com/afis-100-years-100-cheers/

[43] "Inch by inch, life's a cinch", "You can't hoot with the owls at night and soar with the eagles in the morning" and "The only difference between a champ and a chump is U". Cue eye rolls from my kids.

[44] www.dictionary.com

[45] According to ChatGPT the National Association of Home Builders pegs the figure at 3.6 homes over the average homeowner's lifetime, but I can't find the exact source. Let SkyNet begin!

[46] https://www.cnbc.com/2022/02/16/the-average-size-of-a-new-mortgage-just-set-a-record.html

[47] https://www.ncua.gov/files/publications/analysis/industry-at-a-glance-september-2020.pdf

[48] https://filene.org/assets/images-layout/HomEaseOutput_FINAL.pdf

[49] I know about the Federal Home Loan Bank, but I'm trying to keep things simple here smarty pants.

[50] https://www.aacreditunion.org/membership/member-

benefits/#Loan_Discounts

[51] See https://scholar.harvard.edu/dgilchrist/publications/when-31-4-gift-structure-and-reciprocity-field as a clever example of such small gestures.

[52] For all you compliance professionals, let's assume we asked the member if they are gluten or dairy free during the mortgage process.

[53] I'm almost as cool as my dad.

[54] Melina is a former credit union executive and an i[3] alumni

[55] I still made the podium as the bronze medal winner!

[56] For a list of current research fellows, please visit: https://filene.org/about/our-people#fellows

[57] America's Number #1 Buffet Restaurant.

[58] Jello is not a good fit with imitation crab meat.

[59] I'm still not a researcher and this next section may seem flippant to the large group of PhD friends of mine. I absolutely respect your expertise, but my focus is all about application of the research so this section will oversimplify things you've spent your whole life working on and likely infuriate you. Happy reading!

[60] Ms. McKelvey was the first teacher I ever saw outside the classroom. She shopped at the same grocery store as my family and the cognitive dissonance of these encounters stick with me to this day. Didn't all teachers live full time at school?

[61] For all those smarty pants out there, the scientific method does include a few other steps, but you get the idea.

[62] If you've been playing BS Business Bingo, you are close to winning.

[63] Ms. McKelvey's mimeograph is an open source document.

[64] C. Read, "Logic: Deductive and Inductive," London: Simkin, Marshall (1920), p. vi.

[65] He has a branch of macroeconomic theory named after him

[66] The public's most recent experience with the global

health pandemic illustrated the shortcomings of some initial physical science findings

[67] "The Effect of Transformational Leadership at Credit Unions", Amy Colbert, University Of Notre Dame Amy Kristof-Brown, University Of Iowa And Murray Barrick, University Of Iowa, Filene Research Institute, 2006.

[68] Specifically the concept of 'transformational leadership' which is defined as "oriented to making long-term changes in a firm, [by] providing vision and inspiration to employees."

[69] I'll spare you a sample of these tables, but if you are really interested in what these look like give Filene a call.

[70] Some notable exceptions apply including the most recent efficacy results of Pfizer's COVID-19 vaccine.

[71] http://content.time.com/time/health/article/0,8599,1998644,00.html

[72] See www.savetowin.org for details on this program

[73] Fancy word, but practical approach for credit unions.

[74] https://onlinelibrary.wiley.com/doi/abs/10.1002/9781118901731.iecrm0060

[75] https://www.statisticssolutions.com/qualitative-sample-size/

[76] https://sendhil.org/

[77] https://scholar.princeton.edu/shafir

[78] https://scholar.princeton.edu/shafir

[79] Another experiment ideas42 conducted was issue different sized plates to attendees during the first day's lunch buffet and they approximately measured the amount of food the 'big platers' took vs. the 'little platers'

[80] https://blogs.scientificamerican.com/observations/is-smart-technology-making-us-dumb/

[81] Nicolas Cage, who stole the Declaration of Independence.

[82] I'm starting a petition to rename the app Poop Ninja.

[83] Data pulled from https://www.cuna.org/uploadedFiles/Global/About_Credit_Unions/CUMonthEst_Nov20.pdf with

author's calculations.

[84] For a great look at this future I highly recommend my friend Mark Sievewright's book Digital Life

[85] Second chance loans, financial counseling as prerequisite for loans, etc.

[86] Medical debt is a uniquely American (and really stupid) thing

[87] Although not always, see *The Financial Diaries: How American Families Cope in a World of Uncertainty* by another Filene Research Fellow, Jonathan Morduch, a professor at NYU.

[88] This example is necessarily simplistic but you get the idea.

[89] Automobile loans are relatively small and frequent

[90] I love compliance people and I can already hear your concerns.

[91] Nugenix doesn't work

[92] My dad did this as well which I found hilarious when I was a kid. Now I get it. The Progressive Insurance adverts are spot on...I have a fanny pack to prove it.

[93] Substitute 'hate' for 'bother'

[94] https://www.youtube.com/watch?v=MudaxA80eI4

[95] There are a handful of Innovation Man videos I'd recommend viewing. You know how to use Google, so go ahead and find them yourself.

[96] But it is not easy!

[97] Compliance professionals provide a critically important role in credit unions. We could replace compliance with finance, operations, etc. as barriers to early innovation. But come on, compliance is so easy to throw under the bus. Again, I love compliance people, no offense!

[98] Non-paid spokesperson here. Filene has trained nearly 300 credit union professionals in their $i^3$ program and worked with dozens of credit union organizations to teach and implement a powerful innovation methodology over the

past 15 years.

[99] Death threats is a concept borrowed from Doug Hall who runs a wildly successful consultancy and training program called *Innovation Engineering.*

[100] I first heard the term corporate antibodies from Salim Ismail, one of the founding members of Singularity University. Singularity worked with the Credit Union Roundtable, CEOs of the industry's largest organizations, on a project in the early 2010's.

[101] They speak differently than us in Switzerland, thus the non-conforming acronym.

[102] https://www.w3.org/History/1989/proposal.html

**[103]** http://info.cern.ch/Proposal.html

[104] To get a sense of Costas' approach, you can see him in action at https://www.youtube.com/watch?v=PMTZHxgJ9C4

[105] For those keen observers, they did not turn this business book in a Tom Cruise movie about high school football.

[106] The Process of Design Squiggle by Damien Newman, thedesignsquiggle.com

[107] ibid

[108] Creativity and Innovation Under Constraints: A Cross-Disciplinary Integrative Review, Journal of Management, Volume: 45 issue: 1, page(s): 96-121, 2018

[109] "I recognize this example may not age well." - Me, 2023

[110] Apple's Macintosh team flew the Jolly Roger flag as an act of rebellious skunkworks, https://www.folklore.org/StoryView.py?story=Pirate_Flag.txt

[111] https://hbr.org/2019/11/why-constraints-are-good-for-innovation

[112] The Center for Creative Leadership popularized the 70-20-10 model as a heuristic for training and development. Other organizations have taken this model and applied to other uses. For more information visit: https://www.ccl.org/articles/leading-effectively-articles/70-20-10-rule/

[113] Reminds me of a favorite *Onion* headline, "Forward-Thinking CEO Hoping Company Can Capture New Audience By Making Product Worse in Every Conceivable Way"

[114] Not to get too cynical but I'd recommend reading <u>Bullshit Jobs: A Theory</u> by David Graber which postulates that millions of us are caught in jobs that are useless or colloquially referred to as "bullshit jobs".

[115] Let's assume poor implementation =0 and exceptional implementation = 5.

[116] https://filene.org/be-a-part-of-something/labs-i3/flex.one

[117] https://filene.org/assets/images-layout/Flex_One_Business_Plan.pdf

[118] While I'm keen on  sourcing most things, and I'm sure others have different opinions, just go over to https://twitter.com/elonmusk to confirm my hypothesis

[119] https://www.boringcompany.com/

[120] https://sifted.eu/articles/klarna-fintech-raise-650m/

[121] For a great history of consumer credit, visit https://www.library.hbs.edu/hc/credit/credit1a.html

[122] Since 2014, Filene Research Institute has partnered with the Ford Foundation and FINRA Investor Education Foundation to scale this program to more employers and credit unions across the US and you should consider it for your credit union.

[123] Terms are subject to change.

[124] For a nice diversion, check out Professor Sawyer's talk *The Jazz Experience* at https://www.youtube.com/watch?v=i6FZhwUTDSE ... this quote comes at about the 21 minute mark of an hour long lecture.

[125] The dude is amazing, read a bit about his life at https://www.edwddebono.com/about

[126] Probably \Elon, our creative, genius douchebag buddy.

[127] Nearly 1 million managers have been through training provided by deBono's consultancy, so cheesy sounds

153

delicious to me.

[128] https://singularityhub.com/

[129] My second child, Milo, manages me. More about them later, if I can get it cleared through their agent and social media team.

[130] Do any of us really?

[131] Not all the people that reported to me would regard me a good or even average manager, but that's life. I guess it's better to be approximately correct than precisely wrong ◆◆.

[132] Best teacher I've ever seen, check him out at https://news.darden.virginia.edu/2016/12/09/alec-horniman-profile/

[133] pronounced me-HIGH chick-sent-me-HIGH-ee

[134] Flow, Mikhaly Csikszentmihalyi, 2008.

[135] https://www.gallup.com/workplace/321965/employee-engagement-reverts-back-pre-covid-levels.aspx

[136] Compliance people, we have a new scapegoat!

[137] HRIS ... business lingo alert, this acronym sounds like a drunk person saying, "his or hers"

[138] You are the scapegoat again, sorry.

[139] One of the most effective managers I have ever seen is a guy named Michael Neill. He used to be a credit union marketer and for the past 20 plus years has led a sales and service organization, ServiStar, training credit union employees across the US.

[140] Not as nice as The Hampton Inn.

[141] Joe Hearn, current President/CEO from Dupaco, stands out.

[142] Filene had conducted a series of research projects under the domain of COOL Solutions which identified the lack of engagement amongst young adults in all aspects of credit unions.

[143] Yes, the inspiration was Vince Vaughn and Owen WIlson in *Wedding Crashers* ... don't forget Will Ferrell was the original crasher, don't EVER forget that!

[144] "Literally!" - Rob Lowe

[145] http://www.paulschoemaker.com/

[146] https://filene.org/464

[147] The Lake Wobegon Effect, a place where all the women are strong, all the men are good-looking, and all the children are above average!

[148] This report was based on a book published by Schoemaker and his co-author George Day entitled See Sooner, Act Faster, 2019.

[149] For an abbreviated discussion please visit https://sloanreview.mit.edu/article/are-you-a-vigilant-leader/

[150] I'm not a maverick, nor do I sit on the lunatic fringe unless you catch me watching an Everton soccer match.

[151] One could interpret this action as an asshole move, as well. You are entitled to your opinion and trust your instincts.

[152] Check out Member Loyalty Group, a CUSO built to measure NPS in credit unions.

[153] Or today on Spotify.

[154] I personally replace "Terry" with "Carrie" because Terry is my mother-in-law and Carrie is my wife!

[155] Jersey Shore was a bit too far, but same ocean of opaque saltwater

[156] Sorry mom.

[157] http://web.mit.edu/curhan/www/docs/Articles/15341_Readings/Motivation/Kerr_Folly_of_rewarding_A_while_hoping_for_B.pdf

[158] Not the basketball player / coach.

[159] The same year Backstreets was released. Coincidence?

[160] https://www.researchgate.net/publication/291371864_40_Years_After_Steven_Kerr's_Follies_Are_Alive_and_Well

[161] Skinner, a Harvard psychologist, is best known for "The

Skinner Box" which studied animal behavior by rewarding or punishing rats (but sometimes pigeons) across a variety of contexts. Early in his experiments, Skinner didn't find the rats behavior to align with his hypothesis and he famously exclaimed to the rats "Why don't you behave?"

[162] Profits, just say it.

[163] Mike Higgins, Jr. of MHA Stakeholders

[164] Dad Joke, level of difficulty 100.

[165] At least I had one, Dad Joke, level of difficulty 75.

[166] And the later ones too.

[167] Not quite as bad as Michael Scott from *The Office*!

[168] These are not pseudonyms.

[169] My kids, if they are reading this now, are rolling their eyes after hearing these statements for the 100th time.

[170] Keith Richards is an exception.

[171] https://www.amazon.com/Brag-Worry-Wonder-Bet-Managers/dp/1475968744

[172] Peace Corps Volunteer, chief investment officer for a US government enterprise fund in Central Asia, founder of a 1,300 person manufacturing facility in rural Uzbekistan, general manager of a Native American fish processing and marketing organization and now head of community development with Credit Union Strategic Planning.

[173] Right behind Rick Thomas.

[174] https://openpsychometrics.org/tests/IPIP-BFFM/

[175] Despite the fact that we were US government employees in a former Soviet Republic!

[176] Officially we had to get approval to travel by both the Peace Corps and the national government, but this time frame coincided with the first group of Peace Corps Volunteers in country (us!) and the fall of the Soviet Union (yay! No more 'evil empire'). Therefore, everything was a big mess and it was easy to sneak away without anyone knowing.

[177] Married since 1994!

[178] During the Soviet times, citizens had to register with an agency called the OVIR an time they stayed overnight in an place outside their hometown.

[179] Laughable as my nonexistent biceps can attest to!

[180] https://hbr.org/1996/11/what-is-strategy

[181] https://gonzobanker.com/2005/11/gonzo-goes-to-retail-delivery-2005/

[182] For another Porter classic on competitive forces read this gem from 1979: https://hbr.org/1979/03/how-competitive-forces-shape-strategy

[183] https://www.amazon.com/Innovators-Dilemma-Revolutionary-Change-Business/dp/0062060244

[184] Or your "Hannukah Bush" in my case.

[185] https://www.amazon.com/Good-Strategy-Bad-Difference-Matters/dp/0307886239

[186] https://www.mckinsey.com/business-functions/strategy-and-corporate-finance/our-insights/the-perils-of-bad-strategy

[187] My career ended there, no MLS for this guy. Only old man soccer on Sunday's remains on the schedule. The dream is over.

[188] Professor Lerzan Asksoy from Fordham University created a research project and consulting practice around the concept of the "wallet allocation rule" which does a comprehensive job of explaining why it is important to have your brand in a consumer's consideration set.

[189] PSECU and Alliant to name a few

[190] https://www.section4.com/prof-g-show

[191] Props to Sekou Bermiss from UNC-Chapel Hill for teaching me this $100 word.

[192] My other kid, Milo, has received a calling from a higher power to be a dancer, more on them later.

[193] Ask the folks at Enron Federal Credit Union

[194] For example, see <u>Bowling Alone</u> by Robert Putnam and <u>The Unwinding</u> by George Packer.

[195] https://planetpropaganda.com/work

[196] https://www.deepdyve.com/lp/emerald-publishing/strategize-on-a-napkin-CtXXJzn8T0

[197] You can use artificial intelligence and process called sentiment analysis to turn a series of text responses into a summary statement. It's kind of magical.

[198] Start here: https://www.self-help.org/who-we-are/about-us/our-structure

*[199]* He was not trained in marketing, in fact he got his PhD in European History.

[200] https://hbr.org/1992/01/the-balanced-scorecard-measures-that-drive-performance-2

[201] See Jim Gaffigan's rant on British peoples' lack of the use of "the" https://www.youtube.com/watch?v=55HDTtxrqLo

[202] https://www.fdic.gov/analysis/cfr/staff-studies/2020-06.pdf

[203] Think of all the mainline airlines that attempted to create sub-brands to copy Southwest Airlines' low fare strategy and failed.

[204] Co-founder of Generation Investment Management, a pioneer in sustainable investing.

[205] My three favorites are Vancity's Accountability Reports, Clearwater Credit Union's Transparency Reporting and Sunrise Bank's Impact Report (okay, not a credit union but worth a look).

[206] https://link.springer.com/article/10.1007/s10551-011-0948-0

[207] https://onlinelibrary.wiley.com/doi/abs/10.1002/smj.2410

[208] https://journals.sagepub.com/doi/10.1177/0149206314522300

[209] https://link.springer.com/article/10.1007%2Fs10551-015-2671-8

[210] Smith, N.C.; Read, D.; López-Rodríguez, S. Consumer Perceptions of Corporate Social Responsibility: The CSR Halo Effect.

[211] See this report on climate change I recently co-authored for Filene: https://filene.org/learn-something/reports/the-changing-climate-for-credit-unions

[212] https://filene.org/learn-something/reports/amplifying-social-impact-the-state-of-credit-union-giving

[213] Mark Meyer, Philosopher

[214] Simply, then Amplify!

[215] Unknown source, but I'd wager $20 that it was John Oliver.

[216] Non-pecuniary, Sekou!

[217] Though stranger things have happened in U.S. public policy circles!

[218] http://pages.stern.nyu.edu/~adamodar/New_Home_Page/datafile/taxrate.htm

[219] https://perspectives.eiu.com/strategy-leadership/net-positive-new-way-doing-business

[220] https://www.globalreporting.org/gri-20/Pages/Facts-and-figures.aspx

[221] https://www.isc.hbs.edu/Pages/default.aspx

[222] www.ceres.org

[223] www.gabv.org

[224] He has a terrible website www.globalbanktraining.com but you can get his contact information there.

[225] Carrie was horrified that I only brought two pair of underwear.

[226] Ask me someday about a guy named Jesus with a Nazi armband...an unsettling interaction in rural California for this German-Jewish kid from suburban Maryland!

[227] We met up with 3 other individuals on the same route in the middle of nowhere West Texas.

[228] A group of self-described Grannies in their 60's and 70's were on the same route with a support van. We met up about

every week where they lavished us with food, beer and great stories.

[229] We named our group ITC, it's a NSFW acronym and I'll let you guess what it stands for.

[230] See, for example, <u>Microadventures: Local Discoveries for Great Escapes</u>, Alastair Humphreys

[231] Filene Research Institute republished this book in 2008 and can be found at https://filene.org/learn-something/reports/speaking-of-change

# ABOUT THE AUTHOR

**George Hofheimer**

 George Hofheimer advises highly ambitious organizations that want to change the world. He has held executive positions at the Filene Research Institute and CUES. George began his career in international business development, including as a member of the first group of Peace Corps Volunteers in the former Soviet Republic of Uzbekistan. George obtained his MBA from the University of Wisconsin-Madison.

Made in the USA
Monee, IL
10 October 2023

44328743R00095